The Value of a Teacher

THE VALUE OF A TEACHER
IN SEVEN LESSONS

Building up your power and planting
it upon sustainable lifestyles.

Kennedy Onyango Adongo

authorHOUSE®

AuthorHouse™ UK
1663 Liberty Drive
Bloomington, IN 47403 USA
www.authorhouse.co.uk
Phone: 0800.197.4150

© 2018 Kennedy Onyango Adongo. All rights reserved.

No part of this book may be reproduced, stored in a retrieval system, or transmitted by any means without the written permission of the author.

Scripture quotations marked NJB are from The New Jerusalem Bible, copyright © 1985 by Darton, Longman & Todd, Ltd. and Doubleday, a division of Random House, Inc. Reprinted by Permission.

Published by AuthorHouse 01/26/2018

ISBN: 978-1-5462-8432-1 (sc)
ISBN: 978-1-5462-8433-8 (e)

Print information available on the last page.

Any people depicted in stock imagery provided by Thinkstock are models, and such images are being used for illustrative purposes only. Certain stock imagery © Thinkstock.

This book is printed on acid-free paper.

Because of the dynamic nature of the Internet, any web addresses or links contained in this book may have changed since publication and may no longer be valid. The views expressed in this work are solely those of the author and do not necessarily reflect the views of the publisher, and the publisher hereby disclaims any responsibility for them.

Teachers Revalue Ecosystems in the Space!

"Mike Smith, Ellison Onizuka, Judith Resnik, Ronald McNair, Gregory Jarvis and Christa McAuliffe; what was important to Christa, people and their dignity? Her classroom was based on mutual respect. She taught her students to respect themselves too and she taught them to do the very best that they could do and to stay true to their inner selves. Christa stayed true to herself and to the teaching profession. Before the challenger launch, Christa had much work to do, she was training for spaceflight, she was preparing for the space lessons, and she was working with the media, and much, much, more. Christa was also still working with her students, and up through the last day she made time and crew programme to write college recommendations for some of us students. At a time when many would think only of the impending launch, Christa was taking care of the teacher's business. Courage is contagious. Courage is shared. Courage is much more than bravery and boldness because courage lives in the heart. Once

you weigh the risk and once you decide that to explore and to discover are worth the risk, then you can dream, you can plan, and you can build. And then you train, and you train, and you train, and you train. So that when the crew launches, they launch ready, with happy hearts, thankful for the opportunity to represent America, happy to represent history and all of humankind as humankind reaches for the stars. The Challenger crews were wonderful, wonderful people, wonderful human beings. And they were very much like all of you here today."

Barbara Morgan

Dedication

The Value of a Teacher series is dedicated to

THE PUPILS AT CHENGDU'S LONGJIANGLU PRIMARY SCHOOL, CHINA
Who showed their love for and care of the Funan River - 'Mother River' in 1985- After a one-day field study of the river they sent a letter to the (then) mayor, saying: 'We saw residents dumping dirty water and rubbish into the river, wastes were also discharged to the river from a paper mill, a hospital, and a strongbox manufacturing factory, the children appealed to all city residents to stop dumping garbage in the river and to treat industrial refuse before discharging it into the water,' students from other schools followed them -*butterfly effect* "sensitive dependence on initial conditions"- the gift portrait on display in the main lobby of the United Nations Office at Nairobi, showcasing the theme of Green Economy and sustainable development in the context of urban planning presented to UN-HABITAT's Executive Director, Mrs. Anna Tibaijuka from the Mayor of Chengdu in the year 2000, representing yesterday of the fantastic world of quarreling leaders who use human beings as mere pawns, today of partner in the first of the series of plans which lead up to the great strategic planning, and tomorrow leader loving who repeatedly acts to save the

human race even when it fails her - Summer 1859, Jean François Gravelet-Blondin, known as the "Great Blondin," begins a famous series of tightrope walks across the Niagara gorge, the act draws crowds as large as 25,000 people, Blondin crosses in increasingly difficult ways, riding a bicycle, pushing a wheelbarrow and even with his hands and legs bound in chains, his most difficult crossing takes place on August 19, when he manages to carry his manager over the rope on his back;

MY PARENTS
Samuel Adongo and Reene Migen, charts of transformation, who dedicated their lives and businesses to enhance the management Environmental, Social and Governance (ESG) related issues poising risks to companies in Africa though impactful green agenda, Eco-efficiency, planning issuing of green bond and token carbon emissions calculator, Social and Environmental Management System (SEMS);

AFRICAN INLAND CHURCH (AIC) REVEREND JORAM AUMA
Who baptised me on 30 November 1986, '... As long as earth endures: seed-time and harvest, cold and heat, summer and winter, day and night will never cease (Genesis 8:20-22).' According to him: 'the principle of "political, cultural, and *ecological* character of green capitalism" or "Know Thyself" by Socrates, [quoting Greek physicians Hippocrates (460–370 BC) and Galen

(AD 129 – c. 200)] - a proto-psychological theory that suggests that there are four fundamental personality types, sanguine "blood" (enthusiastic, active, and social), choleric "yellow bile"(short-tempered, fast, or irritable), melancholic "black bile"(analytical, wise, and quiet), and phlegmatic "phlegm" (relaxed and peaceful), there are "reasons" for everything we do as human beings to ensure ecosystems brand of climate activism. Henry Martin, missionary to the Middle-East, wrote: "The power of gentleness is irresistible!" Mrs Apunda Pesilla taught me in Sunday lessons - Social and Ecological System Dynamics, an equable climate, an equable temperament "Better an equable person than a hero, someone with self-mastery than one who takes a city" (Proverbs 16:32);

DENISH NYAUGU
A teacher of splendid courage, whocheers how to become smarter at getting a better fit between learning opportunities and the way you learn best, expand 'band width' of experiences from which you derive benefit and improve your learning skills and procession green home designs, [quoting P. Honey] learning styles: activist (learn by doing), theorist (analyze and synthesize actions), pragmatist (practice in the real world) and reflector (take time to work towards an appropriate conclusion) for ecosystem and system thinking approach, including engaging the deaf and hard of hearing in ecosystem conservation - fish and wildlife service;

MY TEACHERS

Who launched revitalization environment education programme and encouraged students to participate regularly in activities to monitor the pollution of the Nyando river "comparing its ecosystem importance to Sheldrick Falls (Kwale, Kenya), Niagara Falls (between Canada and the United States, more specifically, between the province of Ontario and the state of New York), and Victoria Falls (in southern Africa on the Zambezi River)" and campaign for keeping the Dandora landfills clean; and to

KEVIN ALOO

A focused software-defined networking (SDN) professional, whose leveraging of "pollution prevention" and the principle of "ecology first" enhanced my outlook over the 15 year period from 2002 to 2017, impact and its significance through the concept of 'digital conservation', generating more data, faster processing, better information access and connectivity, new communication routes, exciting visual representations and empowering decision-making support systems - data on nature, data on people, data integration and analysis, communication and experience, and participatory governance practices and values.

Foreword

Built on value and planted in value, the World Teacher's Day has been celebrated on October 5, every year since 1994, creating conscience of the value of a teacher in the future of every generation; the book scores the teacher based on three capabilities: enterprise, government and people or civil society. The aim of this book is to respond adaptively to change in case of financial shocks, social instability and natural disaster. There are personal stories like that of the Green chemists John Warner and Paul Anastas who advocate for a fundamental rethink of teaching methods for chemists and designers to issues like toxicity and environmental mechanisms. In the abundance of ecosystems, this book is enabling you to grow firm in authority, honor and ownership of a high definite lifestyle; grasping the earth's breadth and the length, the height and the depth.

Firmly rooted in the value culture, this book draws on the teachers who are revealing themselves to their learners in their love, faith, hope, prudence, courage, justice and temperance; with the leading-strings of wisdom, power and guidance, reflecting all the phases of highly definitive forms of sustainable lifestyle security. It adds that by providing an understanding of a teacher's ability to withstand and capitalize on change, can help governments, policy makers, intergovernmental organizations or international governmental organizations (IGOs), international non-governmental organizations (INGOs), non-governmental organizations (NGOs), civil society institutions, development agencies, investors and private sector enterprise - strengthening a country's readiness for change focused on Mitigation: Transport, Waste, either Energy or Buildings, on Adaptation: Coastal extreme, Social and Economic climate resilience and on Conceptual Planning and Development.

Kagonye Janet Ogata,
Advocate,
The Republic of Kenya

Acknowledgment

The current global debate is dominated by concerns such as poverty alleviation, gender sensitivity, the proper role of the state in sustainable development, the role of macro policies, the role of the human capital in sustainable development and population, environmental and urban policies. These are concerns that statesmen and stateswomen have debated and are actively debating.

In the heart of a statesman or stateswoman lies the value shift towards a more harmonious, balanced and sustainable world. Kenya's 14th Chief Justice David Kenani Maraga, a servant of the mystery, "The greatness of a nation lies in its fidelity to its constitution and strict adherence to the rule of law and above all the fear of God." Tegla Chepkite Loroupe, a Kenyan long-distance track and road runner, a global spokeswoman for peace, women's rights and education.

I received valuable assistance either in person or by studying the life-work of the following of a proud people who have sought to get a predictable, dependable and solid foundation for improved governance across all sectors by focusing on services, innovation, reduced inequality and environmental sustainability:
Prof. Wangari Maathai

Dr. Sally Kosgei	St. Agustine of Hippo
Prof. David Some	Dr James Mwangi
Prof. Bethwel Allan Ogot	Jomo Kenyatta
	Kwame Nkrumah
Prof. Anne Nangulu	Dr. Nicholas Makana
Prof. Amb. Maria Nzomo,	Nnamdi Azikiwe
	John. F. Kennedy
Dr. Paul K. Kurgat,	Dag Hammarskjöld
Prof. Jackson Too	John D. Rockefeller
Prof. Odhiambo Ndege	

Many individuals have pondered what sustainable ecosystem-based adaptation means beyond a simple one-sentence definition. To recall the courage and vision of geniuses, people of stature, who put their lives in danger so that future generations could live as free, this Book bases on five principles of sustainability: Integration application by Chika 'Nancy' Ike, Nigerian actress, entrepreneur and United Nations Ambassador - Refugee Ambassador for Displaced persons and founder of the Chika Ike (Help A Child) Foundation and philanthropist; Mass production and Large-Scale Teamwork by Thomas Alva Edison, was an American inventor and businessman, he is often credited with the creation of the first industrial research laboratory; Innovation by Thomas Alva Edison, was an American inventor and businessman. He developed many devices that greatly influenced life around the world, including the phonograph, the motion picture camera, and the long-lasting, practical electric light bulb; Human Rights and Equity by Ellen Johnson Sirleaf, the 24th President of Liberia, awarded the 2011 Nobel Peace Prize for her non-violent struggle for the safety of women and for women's rights to full participation in peace-building work; and the universal Thomas Woodrow Wilson, the 28th President of the United States, an activist of foreign policy calling on the nation to promote global democracy, he sponsored the League of Nations – the United Nations forerunner; United Nations Environment for Ecosyatem-based Adaptation (green diplomacy).

Contents

Outlook 1
Value #1: Love Builds 54
Value #2: Faith Focuses 82
Value #3: Prudence Integrates 96
Value #4: Justice Explores 105
Value #5: Hope Plans 114
Value #6: Courage Innovates 125
Value #7: Temperance Keys 132
Sustainability 142

Outlook

"Go the significance distance, develop a personal brand insistence, focus your mind on generating nature value. Building up like that - planting the future you want." Reene Jean Flan Kennedy Migen, my mother positioned and connected me, Kennedy Onyango Augustine Carl Adongo, in increasing wisdom and stature and in favor with God and man, as I reached for the dignity and magnificence standout performances. "When I look at the face of the River Nyando I see future political freedom, economic opportunities, and human dignity in the grace of nature; you therefore have to function in the mainstream of the economic light of the nation - creating your own products, markets and finances." Samuel John Bonyo Adongo, my father fondly said.

An ecosystem is a complex set of relationships among the living resources, habitats, and residents of an area. Climate change, also called global warming refers to the rise in surface temperature on Earth. Climate change is happening; Humans are increasingly influencing the climate and the earth's temperature in atmosphere, increasing the greenhouse effect. Greenhouse gases include naturally occurring gases, such as carbon dioxide, methane, and even water vapor.

In fact water vapor is the most abundant greenhouse gas. However, human activities such as traditional rice production releases methane gas that is more than 20 times as potent as carbon dioxide from burning trees or exhaust fumes from vehicles in terms of its warming effect. As the sea ice melts it triggers other impacts, such as the giant iceberg Larsen C poised to break off from Antarctic shelf. A thread of just 20 km of ice is now preventing the 5000 sq. km mass from floating away. Professor Adrian Luckman, a scientist at Swansea University and leader of the UK's Midas Project, said in a statement. Snowcapped mountains and ice sheets reflect radiation away from the Earth - a phenomenon that is known as the albedo effect. This helps reduce the amount of heat absorbed by the Earth, and therefore plays a vital role in keeping the Earth cool.

When ice sheet melts, it exposes dark rock or vegetation that doesn't have the same reflective properties as ice, and thus tends to absorb rather than reflect heat, causing the Earth to get even hotter still. Furthermore, as the atmosphere heats up, so do the oceans, lakes and rivers, which leads to more water being evaporated into the atmosphere. Consequently there is more water vapor present in the atmosphere. This not only contributes to severe weather, but because water vapor is a greenhouse gas, it also contributes to a further cycle of greenhouse effect - warming of the surface and lower atmosphere of a planet. Are you now beginning to understand the knock-on effects?

A value is defined as something worthy of praise and admiration or useful for a determined leadership, innovation, creative industry and entrepreneurship. A teacher with values creates, encourages and sustains dignity, equality and healthy people, planet, prosperity, peace and partnership - the pillars of a world harmony and balance of powers; thinking transformation, spiritual innovation, essence understanding, wise use of time and space.

Value provides an analytical mind, perfect logic and perseverance. Value reveals the flow of healing through unconditional love. Value picks up the vibrations of love to the highest level - universal sympathy. Value stands above the current events for the good of all regardless of colour, gender, race or nationality.

I believe that about 80% of carbon footprint in our various ecosystems is related to values of teachers and learners. Values learnt at school have a long-lasting impact on climate change, disasters and conflicts, environment governance, pollution and resource efficiency throughout life (sustainable building design, renewable energy, waste bottle re-use, locally produced food, waste disposal, green transport, awareness-raising events). See the value pyramid below.

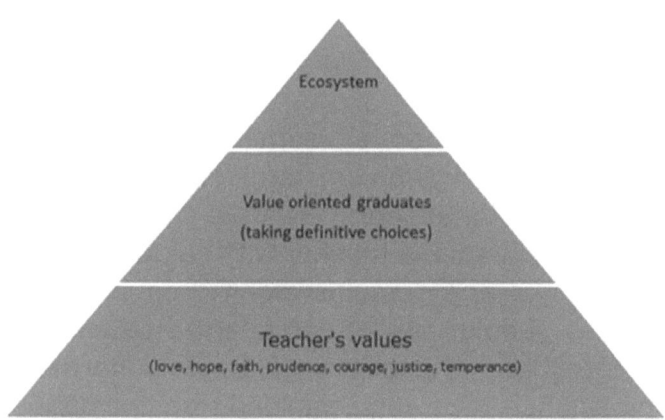

You need to be smart and highly organized to achieve a high definition lifestyle. You need the vision, imagination and proficiency to liberate. You need the passion to negotiate for high end mobility. For instance, the silver cyprinid, it is found in Lake Tanganyika and the Lake Victoria of Kenya, Tanzania, and Uganda. Its local names are *omena* (Kenya), *dagaa* (Tanzania), and *mukene* (Uganda). Being a fast-swimming rather small fish of the open waters, it has been better able to withstand the ecological upheaval caused mainly by the introduced predator *Lates niloticus* (Nile perch) than most other local species. It is not considered a threatened species by the International Union for Conservation of Nature (IUCN). The dried fish is packed in sacks and traders take the fish to the market. A major wholesale market for dried dagaa is in Mwanza, Tanzania, from where it is transported all over eastern and southern Africa for use as food or chicken feed. The family unit participating in Lake Victoria fisheries is important to the long-term sustainability of our Omena as to the Alaska Seafood.

Giraffe is powered by intellect and driven by value. Giraffe sees skyline of the green building home designs; a city built on Green liberalism or liberal environmentalism, liberalism that includes green politics into its ideology. Green liberals are usually liberal on social issues and "green" on economic issues. Green liberalism values the civil servants, judiciary, members of parliament, generality of the people, political parties, youth, women, children, exceptional persons, immigrants, minorities, all churches and religious organizations, members of the defense forces, police and other security services, traditional leaders, and media. I do this with a clear conscience and clean hands: "I fought for the conservation of Mau forest but I was fought politically and I accepted. Right now, we are feeling the impact of failing to conserve the forest. We have seen lives and property being lost in Narok as a result of deadly floods," said Kenya's Prime Minister Raila Odinga. This is one of a few reasons why a *blue-green alliance* is possible in political systems, laws, policies, standards, regulations and processes.

Ecosystem-based Adaptation (EbA) is the management of ecosystems to enhance ecological structures and functions. Accomplished teachers have been making the connections between their work and sustainable development, going beyond theories and experiments to implement viable solutions in creating conducive ecosystem for EbA inquiry; an environment that is promoting and nurturing originality, innovation and quality of practice for ecosystem-based adaptation. Teachers are progressively building a network of highly accomplished learners who understand the need to integrate ecosystem-based adaptation thinking in their daily activities and who are most likely leading future transformations, introducing innovations and creating the foundation for a more sustainable lifestyle within local communities, national, regional and global levels to bring about this shift in scale:

"I am responding first to let you know that if you focus on your goal and work towards it with zeal, however long it takes, you will reach there. Being a teacher by profession, I train to embrace the five pillars of sustainable development: people, planet, prosperity, peace and partnership. You are a teacher too, keep aiming higher, go and do it!" (Jane Safary, Staff Counselling and Welfare Section, United Nations Mission in Sudan)

"Teachers nurture the vision of today's students. In turn, this vision foresees our future. By subscribing to the seven values in the book, and by highlighting the importance of sustainability, teachers help create the right kind of lasting change. I recall fondly the day one of my teachers brought to class a Golden Eagle and through that lesson brought forward the ideas of ecosystem management. This was not only a lesson in facts, but a lesson that helped define who I wanted to be and what kind of world in which I want to live."-Joel Hansen (Deputy Permanent Representative, U.S. Permanent Mission to the United Nations at Nairobi)

"Teachers are indeed the most important figure in a child's life - even more important than the parents' one, I would argue. Teacher is central to achieving the Sustainable Development twin goals: it is a reliable route out of poverty because it has large and consistent returns to income for individuals and because it can drive economic growth. It is also a prime vehicle for promoting shared prosperity. The main challenge in the education sector is to achieve 'learning for all, learning for life'—that is, to ensure that all children and young people acquire the knowledge and skills they need for sustainable lives and livelihoods."-Bianca Notarbartolo di Sciara (Illegal Trade in Wildlife, Division of Environmental Policy Implementation, United Nations Environment Programme).

"Education is not only about knowledge. More importantly it is about values. It is clear that sustainable development requires good education and teachers are the fundamental part, inspiring current and future generations. Current economic crisis and degradation of environment clearly show necessity for rethinking of our societal values." Kanako Hasegawa (Associate Programme Officer for Regional Seas Programme, DEPI, UNEP).

"The future we want is that of learners who have the urge and interest in lifelong learning that will make a change in the society they live in. Hence, it is our responsibility to articulate to students the value of education and this can only be done if we remind ourselves of the values of teachers enriching lives."-Mariam Ayombi Osman (Environmental Education and Training Specialist, Environmental Education and Training Unit, Division of Environmental Policy Implementation, United Nations Environment Programme).

"Personally, the success that I enjoy today I greatly owes it to my teachers because they are the ones I spent most of the time with in my academic life. I only got to be with my parents three months a year, the rest I spent it with teachers molding me, instilling discipline in me and reminding me that the only key to success in this world is education- transforming people."- Linda Chepkwony (President, Africa Focus Youth Initiative).

"I find teachers relevant to the education of all people everywhere, and values such as love and courage that are a crucial priority for the coming Millennium. Teachers, including my own father

Mr. Ogweno of Kowidi primary school made a huge impact on my life for the better." -Wycliffe Ogweno (Administrative Assistant, Chemicals and Waste Branch, Division of Technology, Industry and Economics, the United Nations Environment Programme).

"Having passed through the hands of the late Donald Meda (Xaverian Primary School) and Jeam Agutu (Maseno High School) who nurtured my Mathematics, Agriculture and Wildlife Conservation talents; ultimately by God's grace and supportive [parents, I am a true testament that teachers are indeed vital individual transformative leadership and societal integrative learning. Indeed as postulated by Frank Zappa, 'a mind is like a parachute. It does not work if it is not open.' I dare you to open. I also applaud teachers all across the world for your good work and implore you to continue bringing rays of hope for fulfillment of sustainable development purposes"-Brian Waswala (Environmental Education and Training Specialist, Environmental Education and Training Unit, Division of Environmental Policy Implementation, United Nations Environment Programme).

"I myself have been brought up by a teacher father - Mr. Perseus Mubuta, who is a trainer and great educator both at family level and his contribution in Kenyan society as a Secondary school teacher, Headmaster, Education Attache in the UK, India and Egypt, and eventually working at the Ministry of Education, Jogoo House as a Senior Education Officer up to his retirement in 1998. My Mum has also been a teacher to me, though a Nurse by profession, but she has taught me valuable life lessons. Both sets of my late paternal and maternal grandparents were teachers during the colonial times. My maternal grandfather retained his title "Mwalimu" up to the time of his demise. This was how much teachers were respected. I respect teachers. A special mention to Mr. Gachunga, my Head teacher at Harambee Primary School who never ever forgets his former students wherever we may meet. Indeed, he has even had the honour of teaching some of his former student's children. He taught me Mathematics and Science and enjoyed imparting knowledge. Mrs. D'souza, my High School English teacher at Aga-Khan High School who had such a strong passion for correct spelling and pronunciation. She made me enjoy the English language." Pamela Mubuta (Administrative Assistant, Environmental Education and Training Unit, Division of Environmental Policy Implementation, United Nations Environment Programme).

"My secondary school teachers were my inspiration. The headmaster always reminded me I was an A grade material. This made me to work hard and I made it through Moi University and graduated with a Bachelor of Education (English/Literature) in 2008; now transforming the world through prayer and education at Assumption Sisters of Eldoret. In the Assumption, education is understood as a process by which humankind is freed and sustained." –Sr. Philomena Njeri Karanja (A teacher and Catholic Nun)

"I have to indicate that there are certain teachers who have made me who I am. I rightly mention Mr. Job Bagaka, Mr. Edward Opiyo, Mr. Dismus Oyolo, Madam Ochieng' who also chaired Cheshire Disability Services Kenya, ... People with disability can enjoy life and take part in sporting activities like these children at Oriang Cheshire in Homa Bay County and Prof. Nguyo of Egerton University-thank you. God bless you, God continue to bless Kenya!" - Robert Mwagi (Business Development Manager, National Potato Council of Kenya).

"Greater part of my schooling has been made successful by teachers who were very understanding and who believed in me so much even when I did not see myself as someone who would make it. And most importantly is how professional and qualified they were."-Ruth Aluodo (Sociology and Environmental Study, 3rd year student, University of Nairobi)

"In today's world of information overload, teachers are sometimes sneered at or considered redundant but now more than ever, the teacher's role is invaluable. If imbued with good qualities, a teacher can be helping a pupil sift through the plethora of influences and identify the values that distinguish a compassionate human being from an organism driven by greed." Raza Bashir Tarar (High Commissioner of Pakistan, Nairobi)

Value is the sacred space between a teacher and the ecosystem. Value is source of all life. Value is a sign of generative power. Value enhances reaction time as it seeks to re-orient our plans from fertility window to opportunity window time management wave; reaction based on relationship building - Not Urgent vs important implementation schedule. For instance, I valued the butterfly time in pre-school and Sunday sessions; as dancing improve sense of well-being, enhance stamina and strength, better balance, and makes the body fit. Dancing also elevates endorphin production, thus enhancing the mood in our ecosystems. Dancing also improves cardiovascular health, enhances lung capacity, stimulates the mind to fight Alzheimer and dementia, and increases cognitive acuity, unimpeachable loyalty, meritorious beauty and unflinching character among all age groups. These are the purposes of any sustainable ecosystem cure; guiding the development of 'Going *Green'* culture.

A good case is Curriculum Innovation and Sustainability Thinking by Stirling, S (2004):

Sustainability transition (approach to thinking about sustainability)	Response	State of Sustainability	State of education / curriculum change – curriculum innovation
Very weak	Denial, rejection or minimum engagement with sustainability	No change (or token change) – *change with little difference*	No change (or token change) – *change with little difference* **CURRICULUM CHANGES** Minimal or no changes to curriculum, often content based changes only Teaching, research and community engagement separated out Education *about* sustainability
Weak	'Bolt on' approaches to sustainability	*Cosmetic reform*	**CURRICULUM CHANGES:** Cosmetic changes to curriculum, often content based changes only, limited internally to disciplines, little or no cross disciplinary or inter-disciplinary engagement Teaching, research and community engagement separated out. Education *for* sustainability

Strong	'Build in' approaches to sustainability	*Serious greening*	**CURRICULUM INNOVATIONS:** Environment and Sustainability concerns integrated into all curriculum programmes. Active learning; problem based learning approaches and explicit engagement with values. New forms of knowledge integration (linking practical and academic knowledge in and through active and problem based approaches to learning). Sustainability education
Very Strong	Re-build or re-design	*Wholly integrative*	**CURRICULUM INNOVATIONS:** Inter- and trans-disciplinary approaches to curriculum reform *in addition to* disciplinary innovations. Integration of research, teaching and community engagement to engage pro-actively with sustainability issues and solutions. Transformative learning. Values shift towards sustainability (integrated social justice-ecological sustainability – economic viability perspectives).

In the morning of 8th October 1996, my mother, Reene, handed over the family bible to me and said this is your gift. Read Isaiah 57:14 "Build up, build up, prepare the way, and remove every obstruction from my people's way." I delivered you during the world's devastating drought of 1984. Kennedy means an illustrious leader. As a matter of honour and principle make faith and love your breastplate and hope is your helmet. Be an Essential and a Sovereign man of the community who has the interest of the community at heart. Preside over the restoration of the community and the rebuilding of the ecosystem. Be responsible for the ecosystem regeneration and reform of the community, organizing its security and establishing a sound administration. Set your hands to the good work. 'The God of heaven will grant you success and you, his servant, mean to start building.' Quietly Reshape the World, work hard at it and grow old at your work; a value later noted on 06-06-2016 01:02 PM: "Dear Kennedy, it has been a real pleasure having you in DEPI - quietly going about your tasks with great commitment a very positive attitude. I wish you all the best in your future endeavours." -Mette Wilkie Director, Division of Environmental Policy Implementation (DEPI), United Nations Environment Programme (UNEP).

For many are invited but not all are chosen; it is not enough for you to be a servant, but a light to the nations and reach the remotest parts of earth. So then, increase in wisdom, in stature, and in favor with God and with people. She added: "Your life's decisions should have only one aim: to strengthen trust in the rule of law and democracy." Kenya is generally referred to as "the cradle of mankind." Classically, the enthralling blue waters of the Lake Elementaita well represents the location of Kenya (dark blue); in Africa (light blue and dark grey) and in the African Union (light blue). Like the Classical Music "My Land Is Kenya:

....
My Land Is Kenya
Right from your highlands
to the sea
You'll always stay with me
Here in my heart
Here in my heart

Writer: Roger Whittaker

Kenyan geniuses do not harden or narrow their minds. Their lifestyle is easy, spontaneous and convincing. People of stature are great innovating giants. They are original, self-dependent and create their own principles. Their ideas on the Earth's systems, numbers, and technology are concrete. They conduct the affairs of their community with skill and success. They invest in the right personnel, facilities and equipment. They are experts in planning, preparing, arranging and hosting sales event. They concentrate on profound triumph even when frequented by dynamic failures in

Ahero rice, Sasini Coffee, Ketepa tea, Finlays flower, Muhoroni, Chemelil or Mumias sugar. What we learn from the tragedies of heroines and heroes is not to avoid such tragedies in our lives, but to bear them bravely when fortune brings them. The freedom of your will is shown not in controlling the outward events of your life, but in controlling the inward temper in which you face these events. Your business in life is to paint your doings and manners with critical and strategic acting.

Kenya needs principle-centered leadership with unrelenting commitment to the Kenyan dream of an effective Environmental Management System (EMS) solution, vibrant education sector, perfect healthcare systems, great wealth and efficient transport infrastructure, overflowing with employment opportunities for youth and digitized to the village level. My son, you owe every person you interact with your patience and self-control. Be prudent to recognize your unique position in the universe. Consider it a high privilege and honor to be different from the world. Your evaluation for excellence should be based on utility, relevance and practicability, rather than only on accuracy, reliability and validity; present sound policy reform and development agenda revolving around putting food on every Kenyan's table, water and sanitation, women empowerment, promotion of welfare, and security of and for Kenyans. Inadequate performance cannot be attributed to time and resource limitations. Kenyans will only be persuaded by a corrupt-free and focused leader who can actualize the aspirations of Kenya's independence manifesto of building up a foundation of a society devoid of favoritism, nepotism, exclusion and intimidation of citizenry.

Internationally and nationally, building up promises teaming with experts, professionals, party supporters, trade unions, the entrepreneurs, civil society groups as well as investors in accelerating equal opportunities, democracy, and devolution; campaigning on the premise of economic and social stability, security and national cohesion; valuing equality, social justice, solidarity, sustainable development, gender equality, and democratic security; promoting an open government, increase transparency and deepen democratic reforms; creating wealth and quality jobs for the millions of Kenya's young people; strengthening small businesses and manufacturing sectors in counties to create an inclusive economy and equality.

My feet are tired, but my soul is rested in God's favour. I was named Reene Migen by my maternal grandmother Reene Cherono Migen from the Migen location in Nandi South District. Migen means creativity, curiosity, charm, friendliness, cheer and social life. Thus, I have used my nurturing and helping gifts to serve others in a joyful and accepting way, as a first born of my parents. I have been a master woman, but it was worth it. My hubby was a kind switchboard and a loving man; we always shared the 12 days of Christmas, enjoying the critical freshwater ecosystems habitats and the savanna grasslands ecosystems services, animal games for kids! In Ecosystems and Biodiversity, I have been working with international and national partners, providing technical assistance and advisory services for the implementation of environmental policy, and strengthening the environmental management capacity of developing countries and countries with economies in transition. To enhance Climate Change Adaptation, I have been creating more sustainable communities, workplaces and ecosystems by advancing policy, transforming learning environments, building capacities, empowering youth and women, and accelerating sustainable solutions at local level on the goals and vision of the global adaptation network and related programmes, by supporting deliberations on adaptation knowledge management by the Sulmac Co. Ltd. Throughout my public life, I have been noted for my commitment to mobilize local leaders around a set of new global challenges, from climate change and economic upheaval to pandemics and increasing pressures involving food, energy and water. I am credited with having a determination to see the world deliver tangible, meaningful results that advance peace, development and humanity. You will do well to pay attention to this song *'Happy the Man- Sebastian Temple'* as to a lamp shining in a dark place, with a view to facilitating the development of a stable financial basis for regional adaptation networks, and other intergovernmental processes, as appropriate.

> Happy the man who wanders with the Lord
> ....
>
> Happy the man who learned how to pray
> Happy the man who has a living goal
> Happy the man whose service needs no pay
> This man has found his own soul
> Happy the man, happy the man of the Lord

Kennedy, you would have been swept from the world by drought when you were born or frequenting River Nyando flooding. God has let you survive for this reason: to display his power to you and to have Kenyans talked of throughout the world. Key indicators that lead to happiness are freedom, good governance, health provision and income equality. Kenyans have focused on high-value target lifestyle; Kenya is a country of optimistic people and you are *the authentic* Kenyan.

Here is a teaching that is new, and with authority behind it - that all investments should be led by proper research, planning and organization. You are a special child; everything works together for good. When you find yourself in any limiting situation, handle it with dignity like a bold and brave boy that you are, may be it is in the line of your destiny; whether in values of the fatherland, christian faith and family or ideals of a democratic constitution, market economy and multiculturalism - your reputation at once spread everywhere for patriotism and nationalism. "An admirer of Queen Elizabeth the first, Sir Francis Drake, etched a window at court expressing his fear to declare his feelings, to which the queen left her own etching, saying "Faint heart never won fair lady." Always remember that authentic people find lasting solutions for tough times.

Position yourself in Kenya to preside over high level research and strategy team of experts, communications, resource mobilization, operations and logistics. Graciously accept to play pivotal role in planning and organizing for building up lives and the livelihoods of Kenyans. March forward to bring sustainable quality in depth, speed and rhythm of connecting with Africans and the people of the world. Your little friend, St. Therese, understood that phrase that traced her own destiny: 'At the evening of life, you will be judged on love.' Kenya should develop integrated keenness in Foren Policy and International Relations to realize long-term growth in security, economies and sociopolitical spheres to achieve high sustained lives and livelihoods; be an active and genuine participant in these.

"Our people are resilient. Our people are patient. Our spirits are strong and cannot be broken or outlasted. We hearken to our values. God bless Kenya." She breathed her last that same night, 8th October 1996, at about 2:03 am of malarial depression, just like my father did out of meningitis 7 years before at the Kenyatta National Hospital at 3 am on Wednesday 26th July of 1989. My mother leaves legacy of commitment, creativity and courage in me. My mother heralds an epiphany we can believe in; as a student of the Kabalarian Philosophy - a philosophy of fact and principle.

The family resources were put under Children's Education Trust Fund, with Barnabas Ochoo heading the family trusts. Barnabas worked as an agricultural extension officer with Ahero Irrigation Board and director of the Office of Strategic Partnerships for the Ahero town Department of Education. Barnabas sustained a responsive system in village production, professional networks, technological competence, financial capital and physical capital. The Treetop juice and Ribena that she used to buy for me in Yatin and Format supermarkets in Kisumu City went with her. The English animal story books in which Brain encounters Brain that I enjoyed reading equally disappeared. This did not terrorize me, but my morale rose even higher. It presented with an opportunity to begin my valuable lifestyle: it gave a crescendo and tectonic movement in the weight of my name; I inherited many Swahili, Mathematics and Agroecology books from my elder brother Joshua. From these new fun books, I dreamed of rabbit, poultry (chicken and duck), yellow maize, groundnuts, cassava, sorghum and passion fruit farming, and kerosene (lamp oil) selling. On the afternoon of 12th December 1996, I went to my mother's former friend, Caren Omollo Opuko, to ask for a chore to perform to help me raise money to tart a small business. She gave me a hoe to clear the grass around her son's house. My pay was Ksh. 30. With this boost, I created extra time and extra money from Monday to Friday evening and Saturday afternoon. But of important, I gained the two values: love and courage. With these, I planned on the scope, schedule, execution, monitoring - rescheduling my life game ideologies glacially.

This personal value attracted the admiration of Mr. Onyango Owiny, a Kenya Co - Operative Creameries Limited marketer who invested heavily in a comprehensive *milk* procurement infrastructure to facilitate easy and affordable access to a wide array of extension services from my village "Kodhiambo Village." He gave me a 32 page exercise book worth Kshs 2 to keep record of my agricultural activities under limited marketing to limit so-called resale maintenance. My accurate thinking credentials were further catapult by the competency, proficiency and honesty of Isdora Owade Magada of the Kobudho Community Lake Basin Ecosystem Conservation

Initiative. These finance, investment and fundraising attitudes became very instrumental when I was elected the Treasurer of Moi University Catholic Students Association. While managing the Law of Evidence programmes for the Kenya Military and Kenya Police under Kenya Institute of Professional Counselling/Kenya Institute of Studies in Criminal Justice in collaboration with Egerton and Kenya Methodist universities, I learnt to deal with relevant and important facts in the constantly changing but relatively stable organization of all physical, psychological and spiritual characteristics of an individual which determine his/her behaviour in interaction with the ecosystems. This added to my state of disaster preparedness and competence planning which I had acquired when elected the Vice-Chairperson of the Moi University Peer Counselling Trainining Programme. More so, in transforming Africa through Education Scholarships and Leadership Mentoring under Wings to Fly mentorship programme when I liased and strengthened the collaboration between the Equity Group Foundation and MasterCard Foundation.

Public Service Commission (PSC) State Corporation Advisory Committee (SCAC) and Global Leadership Interlink-East Africa (GLI-EA) Programme Management courses gave me a comparative advantage in determining the destiny of nations through key aspects of project design, planning, implementation, administration and Monitoring and Evaluation; Ways to design, implement, monitor and evaluate projects; Educating Learners on how to link a logical framework and translate it into a concise and transparent budget and a simple work plan; Using the logical framework to design an effective monitoring and evaluation system for tracking and reporting results for individual organizations; and Enhancing best practices techniques for project management, Monitoring and Evaluation.

Later, the World Health Organization (WHO), Holy See, Sovereign Order of Malta and International Labour Orgarnization (ILO) provided me with practical management skills for small businesses:- To buy well, buy: the right quality, the right quantity, at the right price, at the right time; The four Ps of marketing: product, price, place and promotion; Guidelines for better stock control: keep the right amount of stock, stock goods that sell quickly, arrange and display your stock well, check your stock regularly, keep stock records; Different types of costs: direct material costs, direct labour costs, indirect material costs, indirect labour costs; Useful business plans: a sales and costs plan, a cash flow plan; and Steps to follow for cash transactions: prepare your cash box, write down every item you sell for cash, write down when credit customers pay their accounts, keep all receipts for costs, at the end of the day you work out the total cash received, write down all cash sales in the record book, write down all costs in the record book.

Warren Buffet, the second richest person in the world, still lives in the same three-bedroom house he bought in the sixties, and drives himself in an ordinary old car - promoting economically, socially and environmentally sustainable towns and cities - Human Settlements and Adaptation. Buffet is one of the most connected men in the financial world. Types of budgets: operating budgets, deal with planning of activities; financial budgets, deal with cash inflows and outflows; capital budgets, deal with acquisition of worthwhile projects; and contingency budgets, deal with unforeseen events. Principles of financial management: standard documentation; accountability; custodianship; consistency; integrity; non-deficit budgeting; and transparency. This is the "economic citizenship," by making an investment: "In the great fulfillment we must have a citizenship less concerned about what the government can do for it and more anxious about what it can do for the nation." - United States President Warren Gamaliel Harding.

Co-ordinating sustainability on related issues such as Strategic Objective, Tranche, Virement and Economic rent during preparation and implementation of ecosystems-based adaptation. According to the management guru Peter Drucker Strategic objectives are, in general, externally focused and fall into eight major classifications: (1) Market standing: desired share of the present and new markets; (2) Innovation: development of new goods and services, and of skills and methods required to supply them; (3) Human resources: selection and development of employees; (4) Financial resources: identification of the sources of capital and their use; (5) Physical resources: equipment and facilities and their use; (6) Productivity: efficient use of the resources relative to the output; (7) Social responsibility: awareness and responsiveness to the effects on the wider community of the stakeholders; (8) Profit requirements: achievement of measurable financial well-being and growth. Tranche is one part or division of a larger unit, as of an asset pool or investment; the loan may be repaid in three tranches; deal with tranche and manage deficits. Virement is a transfer of money from one account to another or from one section of a budget to another and should be within expenditure or capital, but not across or vice-versa; that the budget virement involves checking the votes which are exhausted versus the ones which have excess funds and ensuring that the total budget remains as it was originally at the beginning of Financial Year (FY); that it is a policy to prepare a budget virement at the end of the 3rd quarter of the FY as a way of reviewing whether you are on course as far as the budget plans are concerned; that the proposed budget is to enable the transfer of budgeted funds from an unspent appropriation category to another, but within one head of appropriation; that transfer will allow you greater flexibility in the use and management of funds and resources to achieve target outputs as specified in respective plans; that proposed budget virement is based on the rule that transfers from capital budgets to operating budgets are not permitted. Economic rent is any excess income that the owner of an input earns over its reservation. The superstars earn large salaries because they have a style or a talent that cannot be duplicated, whatever the training. As Richard Branson may put it, in building your personal brand in marketing you should: look good as the services you provide; put a big price tag on yourself; be trustworthy; prove your worth; and think of yourself as a brand. Changing weather patterns and severe weather events are threatening our development, our security and way of life. "A stable Forex market, a narrower current account deficit and exchange reserves are at all-time high levels which continue to cushion the economy from unforeseen shocks." -CBK Governor Patrick Njoroge. Nuremberg was recently recognized for as the No. 1 Sustainable Large City in Germany. The fruit of the kind of careful numerical analysis value; they projected Sustainability Wheel:

Recurrent Spending: 30%   *Investment: 20%*
Capital Spending: 10%   *Stewardship: 10*
Saving: 20%   *Discretionary Spending: 10*

The Australian Polymer banknotes are banknotes made from a polymer such as biaxially oriented polypropylene (BOPP). Such notes incorporate many security features not available in paper banknotes, including the use of metameric inks. Polymer banknotes last significantly longer than paper notes, causing a decrease in environmental impact and a reduced cost of production and replacement. In the matter of expenditure and receipts; it is not the gift that values most, what values is the natural interest that is mounting up in your account. Fiji selling the world's first climate-change "green" bonds. Poland and France have also issued sovereign green bonds to raise funds for renewable power, subsidize energy-efficient buildings, tree planting and other environmental projects. This is what eco countries look like; fiscal conservatives, but making ecosystem decisions based on facts.

As Dr. Phil., Dr. h.c., Dr. h.c. Baldur Ed. Pfeiffer Honorary Professor of History University of Eastern Africa, Kenya, counseled us during the Moi University 19th graduation ceremony in 2008, a degree is a gift from God to the receiver. So is it a gift or a curse? A gift remains a gift only if it is accepted. It, therefore, follows that a curse is a gift that hurts you. So what ails planet and which graduate strategists could use to advance their agenda as sustainability solution professionals? To start with, let us ask ourselves; what is the world yearning for? On top of my head I know they want affordable healthcare, assured security, food security, good education and infrastructure, cheap and reliable energy and generally a responsive public service. Those issues can only come out if well-articulated in a movement; implementing effective fiscal policies, creating jobs by attracting foreign investors, supporting local manufacturers through reduction of power tariffs, encouraging entrepreneurship by giving opportunities to small business owners like Austin and Amimo Restaurant through low-interest loans, improving the ease of doing business, lowering the high unemployment rate through training and by giving loans for business start-ups, improving agricultural production by empowering farmers and providing more and better extension services, reviewing the agenda for food security and improving it to ensure affordable pricing for commodities, tackling the water shortage in arid and semi-arid regions, lowering the cost of energy by lifting and lowering some taxes, expanding the data communication infrastructure and expanding internet access across the country, reviewing taxes for small and start-up businesses with the intention of making it easy to start and sustain business, and promoting and supporting local manufacturers under programmes such as One Village One Product (OVOP) which was popularly adopted in Japan in 1980's and 1990's and successfully created an economic development model for rural areas.

The objective of value addition should be to kill the virus of unsustainable production and consumption patterns and eliminate all its strains from the body. Only that courage will ensure you have no further outbreaks or incubations and thus infections in the future. Teacher's value is the fastest tool to cure unsustainable lifestyles. My teachers taught me what I refer to as the Frankincense tree calendar. The Calendar: 5 days per week; 8 hours per day; Morning work time 8-12; Afternoon work time 13-17; No weekend working; No holidays in the calendar itself; and a Thumb Rule orientation that work packages should take 8 to 80 hours, while finding a mid-way for work, resources, time and cost. Differences in soil and climate create even more diversity of the frankincense resin, even within the same species. Boswellia sacra frankincense trees on the Arabian Peninsula, in North Africa, and Somalia are considered unusual for their ability to grow in environments so unforgiving that they sometimes grow out of solid rock. The initial means of attachment to the rock is unknown, but is accomplished by a bulbous disk-like swelling of the trunk. This growth prevents it from being ripped from the rock during violent storms. Tapping is done two to three times a year with the final taps producing the best tears due to their higher aromatic terpene, sesquiterpene and diterpene content, the more opaque resins are the best quality.

During his inaugural speech on Jan. 20, 1961, U.S. President John F. Kennedy, a personal hero after whom I named, wasn't wearing a coat or hat in freezing weather as he spoke of beginnings and ends, war and peace, disease and poverty. Deeply tanned in the bright winter light, he stood out against the backdrop of bundled politicians and family. Kennedy started: "We observe today not a victory of party, but a celebration of freedom — symbolizing an end as well as a beginning — signifying renewal as well as change." And he ended with a line that defined a generation: "And so, my fellow Americans: Ask not what your country can do for you — ask what you can do for your country." He touched on inspiration in many ways — "the torch has been passed to a new generation of Americans... Now the trumpet summons us again.... I do not shrink from this responsibility — I welcome it." But none were as direct or memorable as the "Ask Not" line. That was the one that made service an American imperative.

International political economy: When in class seven (1997) Mr. Job Bagaka inspired my interest in agriculture by practicing the agricultural policy of the Swynnerton Plan of 1954. The plan was geared to expanding native Kenyan's cash-crop production through improved markets and infrastructure, the distribution of appropriate inputs, and the gradual consolidation and enclosure of land holdings. Roger Swynnerton was an official in the Department of Agriculture, and the main objective of the plan was to create family holdings large enough to keep the family self-sufficient in food and also enable them to practise alternate husbandry and thus develop a cash income. It was envisioned that 600,000 African families would have farming units of approximately ten acres a family, which would raise their average productivity in cash sales from £10 to £100 a year after providing for their own needs - Ecosystem-based Adaptation and Mitigation, the managing and rehabilitating ecosystems for sustained adaptation to and mitigation of climate change.

In the words of the Special Commissioner for Central Province, 'Thus land consolidation was to complete the work of the [State of] Emergency: to stabilise a conservative middle class, based on the loyalists.' Conversely, government efforts to extend land registration and consolidation to Nyanza stimulated strong opposition preventing the wider development of the wider local bourgeoisie in contrast to the rapid rate of development in Central Province. Nyanza had no such large areas that were well suited to the expansion of cash crops and in much of Nyanza there was lack of high value products on which a faster rate of development could be based.... Nyanza did not stagnate but its marketed output grew much less dramatically than that of Central Province. In regard to the value of a teacher, a seemingly determined attempt to shift priorities is evident. As the Sessional Paper No. 10 of

1965 on African Socialism and Its Application to Planning in Kenya in words of a great teacher President Mzee Jomo Kenyatta…"sets out our philosophy and ideology…defines our course of action…"

Mr. Bagaka bred Friesian cows that are considered among the best in milk production; arguably the most desired dairy breed in Kenya. He also kept African bee species in liaison with African Beekeepers Ltd (ABL), working for the development of the beekeeping and honey industry in Kenya. Mr. Bagaka defined this course of action in me through school banana, carrot, cabbage, onions, Irish and sweet potatoes and avocado farming programme; a greater desire for participation in sustainable African agriculture. East Africa's biggest economy and the world's largest tea exporter, Kenya is a regional hub for companies including Wrigley Company for Youth Development and Environmental Conservation.

Valuing type and scope in the circle of life
As I was waiting for my Kenya Certificate of Primary Education (KCPE) Results, I decided to tour aunt Rhoda Osele's place in Kowuor Centre of Kabondo on 27th December 1998, so she called me next to the fire point where she was cooking maize, she gave a scissor to help trim her hairs. I asked her whether cared for the food. She was in her late 80's. Holding the large grains set in rows on a cob with her cut grey hairs "Do not just live, consider your ways," she

responded. "Live it up, celebrate your Eco post moment, sustainable living, hybrid system, a promise of purity; build and become a smart ecosystem inverter for extra valuable volume for more style," she added.

Now, when I joined high school I discovered that Maize was first domesticated in Mesoamerica, present Mexico, because it was nutritious, easy to store and carry, adapted to diverse growing conditions and provides food and biofuel. A biofuel is derived from a living or recently living organism, as opposed to fossil fuels, which are produced from the organic remains of long dead organisms. Biofuels are used to power vehicles, heat or cool homes. They are renewable than fossil fuels, and better for the environment. They can be made from maize, sugarcane, sweet sorghum and sugar beet. Brazil is successfully using ethanol fuel made from sugarcane.

Later when I frequented hairdressers, beauticians or couturiers, barbers such as Kennedy Okumu of Gravity Haircut, waste pickers, environmentalists, general public and scientific researchers' climate impacts on ecosystems. Human hair is critical areas such as agriculture, medical applications, construction materials, and pollution control. Human hair has the advantage that it is completely biodegradable, renewable, and available in every locality. When human hair waste mixed with compost starts degenerating and mineralizing, it is capable of providing sufficient nutrients to container-grown plants or houseplants and provides similar yields to those obtained while using other kinds of fertilizers and manure. Making soy sauce; human hair is rich in protein, they were able to treat it, remove the amino acids, and pass it off as soybean oil. Hair is also used to make Wig making, Test tress making, Clean-up Oil Spills, Make clothes, Create furniture, Craft a work of art, Nesting material, Crafting a rope. For example, certain communities in China and India have been using human hair to make fertilizers, while certain communities in the USA and Japan have been making ropes from hair for applications in, for example, horse riding (vide infra).

While in form one in 1999, Peter Raburu, the Nyanza Provincial Commissioner recognized me during the school prize giving day as the best student in rapid deployment of drought and disease tolerant seeds to shield communities in arid regions from hunger and malnutrition. "The war against poverty, hunger, food and nutritional insecurity can be won by embracing new and appropriate technologies and knowledge. But most importantly is making these technologies readily and widely available to the people who need them – especially the youth," said Raburu. Kenya has enacted sustainable, climate smart agricultural practices policies while increasing budgetary allocation to boost research on improved dry land crops. This includes application of novel technologies and innovations by farmers such as planting drought tolerant crops like beans, green grams, grain amaranth, cassava, sorghum and millet. At the same time, the Kenya Agricultural and Livestock Research Organization (Kalro), in collaboration with the European Union, and the United States Agency for International Development (USAID), have been promoting adoption of indigenous livestock and chicken that are more resistant to extreme weather events in a bid to boost food security.

In my vision of 'Soaring at the Globe': I made sets of good stretch targets from Nairobi to Victoria Falls to New York; Leveraging on Corporate Social Responsibility to build a trusted brand; Catalyzing Fiduciary duty, skill and care; Impacting Peace and Unity as the bedrock of good governance that propels us to greater heights of performance through almanac, apply or explain principle, strategy, governance, objectives, redesigned leadership planning, high levels of attention and interest, effectively, efficiently and expeditiously in decisions and policies, resources prioritization, directing, monitoring and reporting, I volunteered to teach Swahili at St. Teresa's Opanga Secondary School of Ramba-Kabondo from June 2003 to November 2004. I was ranked the second best teacher of the year in 2004 in the Rachuonyo District by Celine Owuor, the District Education

Officer. Thanks to Madam Antonina Otieno, of Agoro Sare High school, the teacher who made me such a valuable teacher to the world at such an early age.

> *Dear Mrs. Beatrice Okeyo of Otondo Primary school, your focus on promoting ethical leadership and corporate citizenship, corporate reputation and image, corporate social responsibility and investment have been etched in the sands of time. Right now I am doing exactly what you always taught me to do when someone does something that improves your value performance – say thank you. Thank you for confidence and good leadership organization for a broad-based, country-owned process that taps financial and non-financial resources, promotes regional integration, and fosters cooperation among Africa's development partners: the Dedan Kimathi University of Technology - Council Member, which approves the application of University Seal on Graduation Certificates, a notable example, for conferment of Doctor of Humane Letters Honoris Causa (D.HL, h.c.) of Dedan Kimathi University of Technology*

to His Excellency President Thabo Mbeki of the Republic of South Africa on the 6th meeting of the Sealing Committee; pogramme management that Organize the meetings of the United Nations Environment Programme (UNEP), in particular the United Nations Environment Assembly (UNEA, which gave the environment the same level of global prominence as crucial issues such as peace, poverty, health, security, finance and trade); Under the general supervision of the Chief of the UNEP-GUPES Project, I am providing dedicated implementation support to setting the strategic direction of the environmental education programme, programme oversight and progress review and fundraising. According to the logical framework adopted satisfactorily. I work in collaboration with (1) universities and other tertiary education institutions, education practitioners/educators as well as networks (2) government institutions (e.g. ministries of environment, education, and environment agencies) that are supporting education for environment and sustainable *development (3) UNEP and other relevant UN agencies (e.g. UNESCO, UN-Habitat, CBD and other MEAs) that are facilitating the knowledge linkages between education and ecosystems approaches (4) Civil society organizations, including NGOs, youth networks and groups that are participating and supporting active knowledge exchange and networking. I have been assisting in organizing and supporting the meetings of the UNEP Governing Bodies, in particular the second Open-ended Meeting of the Committee of Permanent Representatives (OECPR 2), and UNEA Committee of the Whole (COW2); Draft briefing notes, Chair's scripts, presentations, records and minutes in support of the work of UNEP's Governing bodies; Follow up on meetings of UNEP Governing Bodies; Support communication with Member States and Divisions of UNEP; Carry out protocol functions at the Secretariat; Conduct surveys on client satisfaction and research on best practices being employed by the governing bodies of other UN agencies, governments, funds and programmes and international organizations; and a Coordinator of psycho-social activities; I have been working with socially marginalized groups and individuals by setting up protection mechanisms in order to promote social inclusion. These will help Africa and the world at large to industrialise, but in sustainable manner - For where your treasure is, there your heart will be also. Thank you Mrs. Okeyo for that massive investment of time, energy, health and psychology in reorienting good values in us for building up definitive ecosystem choices in the future - a reflective course of action in supporting environmental conservation measures. Your pupil, Kennedy Adongo*

Kenya's blue sky images and prestige in the ecosystems

The dream of a quality world is our spear and shiled. Through imagination and concentration we organize real world experience into practical usable form. We always look for ways to go above and beyond the expectations of our people. We desire to display and execute vigilant discipline and humble confidence in our works. Kenya's ecosystems provide that chance to develop can-do-attitude: focus on people, do things right, inspire, influence, motivate, build, devise strategy, set direction, create vison, and shape entities for value planning, organizing, directing and controlling. As innovation icon Professor Calestous Juma, the Director of the School's Science, Technology and Globalization Project at Harvard Kennedy Schools; Juma saw biotechnology doing to Africa's agriculture what mobile telephony did to Africa's commerce and to sustainable development worldwide. For instance, Kit Mikayi also known as the weeping rock is part of Mt Elgon and Cherangani hills ecosystem. This has grasslands and woodlands, is a host of Kongoni, Sitatunga, Bongo, Black Rhino, elephants, Reed Buck and Rothschild giraffes. Cheptebo inhabitants of the southern Kerio Valley lived high up on the escarpment with the valley floor used only for the grazing of livestock. Lake Naivasha is a freshwater lake, but it's near neighbour the Lake Oloiden, popularly referred to as the flamingos' paradise and the only world's alkaline waters with tilapia. The lake has magnificent scenery. I have visited all natural lakes in Kenya including Lake Chala and Lake Jipe, located on the border of Kenya and Tanzania. Kenya is the road to manifestation; Sister Anna Ali, A Kenyan Catholic Nun who shed tears of blood every Thursday for 25 years, was born in December 29, 1966 at Kipkelion in Kericho County as the first born child of

Ali Abdulrahmani and Prisca Nyambura. She attended Kipkelion Primary School and Koru Girls near Songhor, Tamu, Muhoroni and Mtetei Valley. Songhor - National Museums of Kenya: The site is situated in Nyando District, Kenya. The site was gazzetted in 1982. It is 78 acres in area. It is a Miocene site dating back to about 19 million years ago. There were a large variety of animals living there. The fossil hominoids collected from this site range from small to bigger apes. Eight species of hominoids have been identified. There is enough evidence that the proconsul africanus also lived at this site. Industrial Minerals Project (1981-1986), a joint Kenya-Finland Technical Cooperation project assessed limestone deposits for cement manufacture at Koru and Songor. Morning View Coffee House and Roastery go to the pool at the Beach Klub at Koru Village to enjoy the beautiful day; a unity, tolerance and strengthening of family - pathways promoting co-operation, scientific research and information exchange for sustainability.

Higher Education Sustainability Initiative overview

The international and regional have progressed in the areas of the leadership and strategy; modeling practice; education and learning; partnerships and outreach for sustainability in Higher Education.

Modelling practice Across Campuses: Sustainability efforts to minimize waste and energy consumption; develop low carbon buildings; protect biodiversity and natural space; source sustainable goods and services; and model sustainability to influence behaviors of staff, students and local communities.

Research for Sustainability in Higher Education: To be more inclusive of: research that is inter- and-multidisciplinary, research that has social impact, research that transforms, research that focuses on social and structural change, researcher as partner, research with people. Asia-Pacific is a good case study under "ProSPER.Net"; not beneficial only to elites: owner-employers, best-funded candidates, high-ranking politicians...

Education and Learning for Sustainability: Moving towards: innovation within existing curricula; questioning and getting to the root of issues; encouraging clarification of existing values; seeing people as change agents; creating opportunities for reflection, negotiation and participation; challenging the mental models that influence decisions and actions; and more focus on professional and social change; constructive creation of alternative futures; and learning to change are taking place world-wide in universities such as Plymouth State University.

Leadership and Strategy for sustainability: Most universities are fully committed to exercising sustainability leadership in the area of administration and finance. They are also committed to environmental literacy and the practice of sustainability via the Talloires Declaration. In Kenya, University of Nairobi has designed Environmental Management System. This value means that, fundamentally, some form of real democracy is maintained, with the citizenry able to hold educationalists to account for the common good, through responsible governance: One, a Master Plan that pledges to foster nationhood by ensuring creation of more vibrant industries and putting in place financial austerity measures to avoid abuse of public funds; two, a manifesto focuses on key sectors such as education, health, security and social safety nets, business, social care and infrastructure.

INNOVATION IS KENYA'S MT ETNA

Research: Main reasons for food-related greenhouse gas emissions: Fertilizer production and use, irrigation, tillage, machinery, livestock, land conversion, cooking, cleaning, transport, cooling, and leftovers. Hybrid rice will boost Africa's production. Use of high yielding inbred and hybrid varieties can boost rice production in Africa, AfricaRice, the continent's main rice research body, says. While the continent's rice production averages two tonnes per hectare with Nigeria being in the lead. Egypt's production is nearly 10 tonnes per hectare, one of the highest globally. We have best rice in Kano States of Nigeria and Kenya. "Hybrid rice is also more competitive with weeds, a major constraint, particularly in direct-seeded rice," said Raafat El-Namaky, a hybrid rice breeder at AfricaRice Centre. El-Namaky said hybrid rice also help African rice farmers get used to certified seeds because it is necessary to renew the seed every year to reduce methane emission [Misheck Mwangi].

Curbing wastage of building materials by Milliam Murigi: Rose Muigai is the founder of the Ballast and Construction Dust Company Limited; the firm is currently operating from Ruai in Nairobi, with a sales office located along Ngong Road near Kenyatta National Hospital. They package more 1,000 bags per day. "I started out with Shillings 140,000 and this amount was enough for me to pay for first set of bags, buy the ballast, weighing and sewing machines as well as labour costs," she said. Rose says that even if many people plan and calculate the quantities of building materials they need, a big percentage buy excess supplies because, currently, construction materials are sold in bulk. This is why on every construction site, there must be wastage and as materials such as ballast and sand cannot be stored easily and most of it ends up in landfills.

Mortar and pestle approach to hycinth: Lake Victoria is a wide natural resource. Her massive bowels have continued to churn out tonnes of fish over the years. In other words, the lake is a massive aquaculture centre, with no apparent agricultural process. And then, a few decades ago, the lake lost its silver reflection. In its place came a rapidly encroaching plant that covered the surface: the water hyacinth.

ClimateCare:

Toyota has announced it will test electric cars in Japan from 2020 equipped with artificial intelligence to help the cars better understand and adapt to their drivers. A driverless concept car, the Concept i-series, can also be driven manually.

Jaguar Land Rover has become the latest large carmaker to say it will stop launching new models solely powered by internal combustion engines, two months after Volvo pledged to do so.

Toyota and Jaguar have promised that all new models from 2020 will be fully electric or hybrid, a year later than Volvo's target, but a big step beyond its unveiling last November of a single electric concept car is *ClimateCare solar initiatives in Kenya*.

Energy Education and Environmental Design:
A green home is a type of house designed to be environmentally friendly and sustainable. In general, a green home is a type of house that is built or remodeled in order to conserve "energy or water; improve indoor air quality;

use sustainable, recycled or used materials; and produce less waste in the process." This may include buying more energy-efficient appliances such as solar panels and other solar-powered devices or utilizing specific building materials that are more efficient in keeping both cool and heated air inside the structure, insulation materials, and protection of natural resources: Straw Bales, Grasscrete, Rammed Earth, HempCrete, Bamboo, Recycled Plastic, Wood, Mycelium, Ferrock, AshCrete, and TimberCrete.

The 19th Session High-level Committee on South-South Cooperation in Nairobi, Kenya: The 19th Session of the High-level Committee on South-South Cooperation met in May 2016 to review progress made in implementing the Buenos Aires Plan of Action, the new directions strategy for South-South cooperation and the Nairobi outcome document of the High-level United Nations Conference on South-South Cooperation. The 19th Session featured a thematic discussion on "the contribution of South-South cooperation and triangular cooperation in the context of the 2030 Agenda for Sustainable Development" on 17 May. Diplomats and development practitioners participated in the thematic discussion, led by prominent panelists representing United Nations organizations and agencies, development banks, academia, the private sector and civil society.

Paris Agreement in Kenya: As of April 2017, of the 143 countries that have so far ratified the agreement, 33 are in Africa, including Benin, Burkina Faso, Cameroon, Chad, Ethiopia, Gabon, Gambia, Kenya, Nigeria, Somalia, Tunisia, Rwanda, Uganda and Zambia. That is 60% of the total number of African countries. Beyond the ratifications, many countries have also fulfilled a key requirement in the agreement by formulating their Nationally Determined Contributions (NDB).

According to the World Bank, there are more mobile phone users in Africa than the U.S. or EU. Since 2000, mobile phone usage grew from 16.5 million to 650 million people. Kenyan women, have launched a new mobile application as part of its efforts to empower both rural farmers and women seeking careers in technology. The original M-Farm SMS tool was launched after winning the IPO48 competition, a 48-hour boot camp event where web and mobile startups competed for €10,000 ($12,242) of capital investment. The business was founded by three young Kenyan women – Susan Oguya, Jamila Abass and Linda Kwamboka – who met through the iHub in Nairobi. Their award-winning idea was developed at the m: lab incubator in the same building. It already has over 5,000 subscribers, having started in November 2010. Africans are impacting the world and taking control of their own destiny by partnering to achieve Ecosystem-based Adaptation. BF Suma Pharmaceuticals in Kenya; it was established in the United States. It is a health product company dedicated to research and development, manufacturing & distribution and consistently providing natural yet high quality products to benefit the health and well-being of people. The Tel Aviv in Kenya; Israel based startup firm Mobile ODT, launched by Ariel Beery and David Levitz in 2012, develops and manufactures a relatively inexpensive and portable diagnostic tool combining the power of biomedical optics with the computational capabilities and connectivity of mobile phones for detecting cervical cancer. The EVA (Enhanced Visual Assessment) System's connectivity, workflow assistance, and remote consultation platforms enable any health provider on the planet (23+ million) to perform expert-level visual-based diagnosis to catch disease early enough to treat. The Prime Minister of Israel, Benjamin Netanyahu and highlighted Israeli innovation in Africa and developing countries. Several Israeli companies changing the fields of health, agriculture, and education presented on their work in Africa.

THE ECONOMICS OF ECOSYSTEMS AND BIODIVERSITY

"A hero is born among a hundred, a wise man is found among a thousand, but an accomplished one might not be found even among a hundred thousand men." -Plato. When I was still a youth, before I went picking *Cactus Aloe* in Kano Plain, I desired to build me up accomplished man in Kenya's Kano Wind Power, cowpeas, sugarcane, tomatoes, sorghum for local consumption while rice and cotton for export and industrial purposes, and hides and skins – catalyzing mitigation of climate change, disasters, conflicts, chemicals, waste, and leveraging environmental governance and resource efficiency.

As William Samoei arap Ruto, the Deputy President of Kenya, would encourage Kenyans to do much more in agro-based processing to increase Kenya's export business volumes, ensuring that airlines do not drop off passengers or cargo at Kisumu or Eldoret International Airports and return empty; the David Ben Gurion's dream of filling Israel's barren hills with trees. Carob trees only have fruits after 70 years, so there is the story in [Jewish tradition] about an old man who asks a farmer, why are you planting a carob tree if you will never enjoy it? And the farmer says, my father planted a carob tree so I can enjoy it, and I will do the same for my children. The symbolism is that all of our interactions with nature should really be about protecting them and keeping them whole for the next generation.

Mahatma Gandhi rightly noted, South African Aloe, Greek, Italian and Arbequina Virgin Olives, Arizona Mesquite, and Thailand Tea Tree Oil for Tetmosol soap are trees of peace, beauty, drought resistance, and classic association; A nature-based response to Youth Development and Environmental Conservation. To see young people organizing Ecosystem-based Adaptation through social media is constructive, facilitative and solutions-oriented; *Tête-à-tête* representing, protecting, negotiating, ascertaining and promoting sustainability - teaching is by all accounts "a most splendid affair" to royals and dignitaries from all over the world. Cultures of act fast, keep things simple, just do it and think out of the box; Market Forces, Fortress World, Policy Reform and a Great Transition to market-driven world in which demographic, economic, environmental, and technological trends are sustainable.

I am a *Kenyan Cactus Aloe* with a dual mission: to preserve environment "unpolluted"; and to maintain it "for the enjoyment, education, and inspiration of this and future generations through watershed protection, erosion control, fire management, and carbon sequestration.

Value #1: Love Builds

Bertrand Russell describes love as a condition of "absolute value. In grades kindergarten to third, new information is presented to us kinesthetically; grades 4 to 8 are visionary presented; while grades 9 to college and on into the business environment, information is presented to us mostly through auditory means, such as lectures - you ignore love, it trends; you allow it to speak, it takes the show; you silence it, it support grows louder; you throw stones at it, it builds a foundation for Quality Based Selection (QBS). As *Martin Luther King, Junior* aptly puts i*t - We* must discover the power of love, the power, the redemptive power of love. And when we discover that we will be able to make of this old world a new world. We will be able to make men better. Love is the only way. Jesus discovered that. Not only did Jesus discover it, even great military leaders discover that. One day as Napoleon came toward the end of his career and looked back across the years— the great Napoleon that at a very early age had all but conquered the world. He was not stopped until he became, till he moved out to the battle of Leipzig and then to Waterloo. But that same Napoleon one day stood back and looked across the years, and said: "Alexander, Caesar, Charlemagne, and I have built great empires. But upon what did they depend? They depended upon force. But long ago Jesus started an empire that depended on love, and even to this day millions will die for him." Kennedy Onyango Adongo is a go forward regional leader; confidently showing leadership, upholding international law and using relations in creating onward opportunities for our people, obeying both the time and space sustainability frontiers.

Friday, May 18th 1984 at 10:00 GMT +3, in a middle-class ecosystem, I was born Kennedy Onyango Augustine Carl Adongo in Ahero Sub-District Hospital, a Government Public healthcare in Ahero town, located next to Ahero Police Station, crossing the River Nyando, along Kisumu Busia Road, Nyanza, Kenya. I spent most of my early life in Dandora Phase 5, Nairobi, Kenya. I am the second and middle son of Samuel Adongo Ochieng' (1944–1989), a logistician with the Kenya Chamber of Commerce; blended together with Kassim Owango started Common Market for Eastern and Southern Africa (COMESA) and with Kassim as the Chairman of Trade and National Chambers of Commerce, they made the Department operational and resourceful. They also started and facilitated the Export Processing Zone (EPZ): Kenya's special Economic Zones for sustainable business opportunities that presents the best opportunity for growth, development and wealth creation; An important feature of ecosystem-based adaptation has been the rapid expansion of EPZ throughout the world. They were also shareholders of Milligan Company; they saw the removal of water hyacinth in Lake Victoria with Mr. Neil Robertson who was the project Manager. A lot of funding has come from the World Bank, Egypt, NGOs and China in millions, but the problem has never been resolved. Reene Migen (1950–1996), my mother, was a field controller with Sulmac Co Limited; A collective Economic Partnership Agreement signed by the East African Community (EAC) states of Kenya, Tanzania and Uganda region allows duty free access of vegetables, fish, and flower exports from the local industries to the European market - Economic Partnership Agreements (EPAs) are trade and development agreements negotiated between the European Union (EU) and African, Caribbean and Pacific (ACP). Under the EPA, increased trade with EU in horticulture could have a protection of fragile ecosystems such as coral reef and health protection from harmful agrichemicals - as commercial fertilizers, pesticides, and feed supplements: Underscoring the importance of harnessing technology for development, addressing the widening technological gap and the growing capacity-development needs with regard to implementation of sustainable development programmes in the East African states; all of which requires formulating national scientific research and technology policies, improving the quality of education and building a knowledge society, raising levels of investment in research and development and innovation, promoting regional cooperation, supporting the establishment of an international mechanism for facilitating the development, transfer and diffusion of environmentally sound and clean technology to developing countries, and reconsidering the current forms of cooperation in technology transfer, indigenization and financing, including South-South partnerships.

Gradus with his wife, Bamburi beach, Mombasa. My maternal grandfather was Hezborn Ondieki, a merchant, Ngong, Nairobi, Ondiek whose descendants rooted from Mangere Sub-location in Gucha - Kisii; paternal, Gradus Ooro, a wildlife tour guide, Mombasa Marine National Park (Kenya). The park lies between the Mtwapa and Tudor Creeks and its blue waters are ideal for windsurfing, water skiing, snorkeling, swimming and diving. They also provide a home to a colourful variety of marine species including crabs, starfish, stone fish, cucumbers sea urchins, corals, turtles, sea grasses and interesting migratory birds including crab plovers. My ancestral heritage includes Luo, Kalenjin, Kisii, Kikuyu and Luhyia. I am grateful for the diversity of my heritage. So our unity comes from somewhere different, not from place or tribe, but from our values and shared commitment to one another. Those values of equality, freedom, democracy, human rights, social justice and the rule of law are the backbone of our society; fight for elimination of gender discrimination in laws, customs and practices related to land and property. The constitution also provides for encouragement of communities to settle land disputes through recognized local community initiatives without hate on ranch owners; ensuring equitable access to land, securing land rights, transparent and cost effective administration of the resource. We must continually re-commit ourselves to working for them, and for the idea that what unites us is greater than whatever may divide us. Our diversity is our strength. Kenyans are a people of many identities and many histories, but share the same commitment to one another and to a shared prosperous future. Kenya's democracy, its vibrant and free media, its lively civil society and political debate are enormous strengths. Election years in our country mean new direction, new policies, and new impetus, regardless of whether a government is new or returning. Kenyans share a history, with moments of great joy and of deep pain. But it has created between us a fabric of connection that still binds us together today, and binds our futures together too. Our partnership is in strong shape – in trade, investment, tourism, development, security and defence, in the links between our peoples and in our common commitment to resolving the challenges of this region, including the conflicts in Somalia and South Sudan. Kenyan stand today as diverse, vibrant, globally-connected people, engaged with each other and with the world. I am confident we will continue to work together to tackle the challenges we face, to bring greater security and prosperity to our people.

In September 1986, my mother transferred to work in Naivasha. I moved to our home in Ahero to live with my step-mother Esther Adhiambo Adongo, a committed mother dedicated to raising the family's eight children: half-brothers George (the climate change witty boy who planted blue gum trees in the 10,000 m^2family land in Kochogo location) and Moses; half-sisters Rose, Lillian and Beryl; and full-brothers Joshua and Elvince; including early years in a communal house, shared by several families, who lived in a traditional fashion, with more distant relatives often visiting. I lived a carefree childhood, spent in village with my maternal grandmother Rosa Midiany joining my paternal grandmothers: Rose Adongo of Sidho (joka KOMBE KOMBE or jo-Kisii), Wilfrida Adoyo, Leukadla Aomo of Luhya clan, and the great grandma Sabina Nyambura "Ombura" a Kikuyu of the Siboga Nyamawa community in Muhoroni were deeply ecosystem caring ladies who towered Kenya's landscape singing the East African Community Anthem "One People, One Destiny":

1. Ee Mungu twaomba uilinde
Jumuiya Afrika Mashariki
Tuwezeshe kuishi kwa amani
Tutimize na malengo yetu.

Jumuiya Yetu sote tuilinde
Tuwajibike tuimarike
Umoja wetu ni nguzo yetu
Idumu Jumuiya yetu.
......

On 30 November 1986, I was baptized by Rev. Joram Auma of the African Inland Church, but converted to Roman Catholicism traditions, as a young man I gained a reputation for being cool to others and absorbed early the influences of Kenyan leaders from my village such as Charles Obinju Opuko, Director General of the Kenya Maritime Authority who introduced remarkable fiscal discipline and monetary policies that ensured sustainable maritime environment and scarce living resources. From Charles came attributes of leadership on the platform of peace, prosperity, and conservatism. These ranged from the moral categories of "crisis leadership," "moral authority," "pursued equal justice for all," to the more technical ones of "economic management," "administrative skills," "performance within context of times," and "setting an agenda." She combined strength with courage gentleness, tenderness, and great unselfishness.

Esther, my step-mother, sent me to Kagimba elementary school where I was taught by Mrs.

Omoro Susan; here I proved to be an adept pupil. Susan would not tolerate in us children selfishness, cruelty, idleness, cowardice and untruthfulness.

I attended Kagimba Primary School from kindergarten through class 6, starting in May 1988. In 1992, at class 2, my admirer, deputy head teacher Mrs. Odera Pamela, who was one of the first to discover my literary talent, taught me the stories of African leaders such as Kwame Nkrumah of Ghana, Nnamdi Azikiwe of Nigeria, and Jomo Kenyatta of Kenya who pioneered environmental justice movements across African continent to promote global relations within the framework of the United Nations, in order to better protect the interests of threatened peoples and the ecological systems in which they are embedded, and upon which their survival depends left an indelible impression on my mind. My early self-identification with Truth and Love as supreme values is traceable to my identification with these leadership stories. In 1993, I progressed to class three having attained position one as the best in English as well, and eventually became a class prefect- a perfect start.

The Nyando River, which traverses the Kano Plains and covers a large area of the lower plains, is the most notorious for frequent flooding. Kano plains have black cotton soil which is very fertile. Thus, the socio-economic characteristics of the community are centred there - including fishing, irrigated rice cultivation, sugarcane farming, cotton, flower, mango, orange, papaya, sorghum, tomato, and pease (for pudding) cultivation. Kano cotton cultivation is supporting the Kisumu Cotton Mills (Kisumu), Rivatex East Africa Ltd (Eldoret), and African Cotton Industries (Mombasa) for research, product development, extension and production. Despite the great potential Kenya has in cotton production in Kano, Embu, Meru, Lower Kirinyaga and Tharaka Nithi areas, its cultivation is not well explored to transform the rural economy. This calls for entrepreneurs focused on diplomacy and financial to change the composition of their investments like Peter Munga who is buying ginneries such as Meru Ginneries and revamped it and contracting farmers. To add value, Peter is manufacturing sanitary towels and diapers. Kenya does not to import these necessities while we can make them locally and sell affordably. The textile industry in Kenya has a lot of opportunities because currently the country does not meet its quota in the African Growth Opportunity Act opportunities to the market in America. Besides cotton seeds, he also produce groundnuts, sunflower, maize and vegetables for commercial purpose. ANGOA, also referred to as the United States Sub-saharan Africa Trade and Economic Co-operation, gives a chance to African countries to trade with the US under preferential treatment, mainly tax-free.

Yams have compounds that stimulate the ovaries. Yes, wild yams. Papaya and guava improve your lifespan. Fish keep your arteries well-oiled. Porridge mops up cholesterol, helping keep your blood vessels smooth and stretchy. Bananas keep sodium low and reduce pressure. Hard women take a cup of black tea a day to reduce ovarian cancer. Hard men take a cup of coffee a day. On a global basis, cassava is ranked third most important healthy food.

River Nyando is one of the major Rivers in the Lake Victoria Basin. It has the third largest River catchment (3550Km^2) after Nzoia (12842km^2) and RiverKuja-Migori (6,600Km^2). It has its source originating from the Nandi and Tinderet Hills in Nandi County and Londiani and West Mau Forests in Kericho County and has a total length of about 170 km. River Nyando is a major contributor of sediment, nitrogen and phosphorus to Lake Victoria from domestic and industrial wastes, and from farms (agro-chemicals). Out of the 170Km of the river, 100km of the riverbanks are bare (no vegetation).

According to our forefathers, Kano meaning is attributed to power, wisdom, security and guidance based upon intelligence, love, self-control, gentleness and patience; it warns that where jealousy and self-ambition exist, there is disorder and every foul practice resulting from fear, ignorance and superstition. Nyando meaning is connected to resource-rich, confidence, assertiveness and creativity; it shows our social and economic development, stressing environmental education, public education, public hygiene, community health and residential facility goals which we must achieve to become the best versions of ourselves. Hence, the community's greatest belief is that strong and united families make up the environment and a well-coordinated country which results in a developed nation. Ahero (meaning peaceful partnership) is located 20 Kilometers east of the Kisumu (meaning a place to look for food) county capital. Two major roads meet at Ahero, the B3 road from Nakuru to Kisumu and Isebania-Kisii-Ahero Road, bitumen standards include spacious paved shoulders, climbing lanes, footbridges, an overpass and other other features designed to promote road safety, the road form part of the A1 Road, which connects South Sudan to Northern Tanzania through Kenya. The Nyando River flows through central Ahero and helps irrigate its many rice fields. In Kenya, Kano is known for fertile black cotton soils. Kochogo, meaning «great King,» a title applied to the first kings, in my case, Kochogo-North sub-chief, Peter Ochieng' Kadu, such a kind paternal uncle – a tactical and strategic leader.

The river's annual flood season is March to May with a peak in April. The climate varies from the hot humid dry low lands to cool wet climate of highland river source. Also River Nyando shares its headwaters with other basins in the region such as Gucha and Mara basin. Additional heat stress, shifting monsoons, rising temperatures, changing rainfall patterns, drier soils and river water level rise are perhaps the most severe threat to livelihoods. The River Nyando floods have sometimes become frequent and unpredictable, as a result of this, in April 1993, River Nyando busted its banks and the whole school was being sucked violently downward. I instinctively clung on to a small guava plank and the next thing he recalled was the splash of an oar as he lay at the bottom of a small boat by uncles Charles Begi, Daniel Ooro and Paul Ramji, and mum Susan from the Bukusu community.

In 1993, second term, I dropped out of class three at this time for one term due to these frequent floods from the River Nyando. Many living thing on the face of the earth was wiped out, people, animals, creeping things and birds; they were wiped off the earth. Little by little, the waters ebbed from the earth. After a hundred and three days the waters fell. The waters gradually fell until the earth was dry and fresh olive leaves thrived again. The surface of the ground was dry, the school was opened, and it was third term. Clinician Kepher Nyaranda and Miss Rose Nyaranda led us in community cleaning after the flood; Mrs. Okiro who challenged me to be unlimited man by narrating the story of Joseph.

Mrs. Okiro Margrate, A TEACHER OF INDOMITABLE VALUE: "The blessed and only potentate (=God). Religion, of course, does bring large profits, but only to those who are content with what they have. You must aim to be upright and religious, filled with faith and love, perseverance and gentleness. Fight the good fight of faith and win eternal life. Do well and be rich in good works, generous in giving and always ready to share-this is the way you can amass a good capital sum for the future if you want to possess the only life that is real. My dear pupils, take great care of that has been entrusted to you. Turn away from godless philosophical discussions and contradictions of 'knowledge' which is not knowledge at all; by adopting this, some have missed the goal of faith. Grace be with you." She made me realize that success is very largely a matter of adjusting one's self to the ever-varying and changing environments of life: increase in air and water temperatures, changing precipitation patterns, increase in the frequency and magnitude of extreme weather events with long term negative effects on many sector, in a spirit of harmony and poise. Harmony is based upon understanding of the forces constituting one's environment; therefore, this chapter is in reality a blueprint that may be followed straight to success, because it helps the student to interpret, understand and make the most of environmental forces of life.

Usually, in rural public schools pupils in lower classes go back home after morning classes. Having recognized the disturbance caused by flood to her pupils, Mrs. Okiro organized with our parents to allow us back in school in the afternoon. Our parents agreed to it. But instead of using this time to teach us the uncovered lessons, she used it to tell us the Bible story of Joseph the son of Jacob. This is a first start at looking how to better integrate lessons of science, climate and practice to foster sustainable rural communities. The objective was to improve the quality of teaching and learning by restructuring the course for Climate Change and Adaptation to include the direct involvement of pupils with local communities. Mrs. Okiro helped me to demonstrate toughness and courage in the most difficult situations, including disasters. Building on the confidence of Mrs. Okiro, I began leading the cleanup of villages, schools and hospitals after the floods.

"What is necessary to change a man is to change the awareness of himself," Abraham Maslow. Joseph's Coat of many colors in a song as sung to the class under a blue gum tree by Mrs. Okiro:

Coat Of Many Colors
There were rags of many colors
....
Momma sewed the rags together
....
As she sewed, she told a story
From the bible, she had read
About a coat of many colors
Joseph wore and then she said
I hope this coat will bring you
Good luck and happiness

(Dolly Parton, 971)

Mrs. Okiro said that just like Joseph, if you focus on your goal and work towards it with zeal, however long it takes, you will reach there. She continued:

POEM ON YOUNG JOSEPH, THE DREAMER

Young Joseph dreamed. In the daytime too,
he would dream,....
......
Down the road were his twelve brothers
with one blood at the fracture of his dream.

....He sank deeper and deeper into his pit
and was sold to wind and strangeness. ...

Joseph, the dreamer, whom many held in awe.
Yair Hurwitz(*Mandatory Palestine, 1941–1988)*

The poem was fascinating, made me think more deeply. To my amazement, I began to enjoy listening and reading as the stories and songs of Joseph gripped my imagination and I became a young person with ambition and direction. I was down to number 10 that term. "All our dreams can come true, if we have the courage to pursue them."-Walt Disney. My outlook underwent enlargement in time and I regained my position one by the end of term one of class four and was made the class prefect. My thought having attained a consciousness of itself and its worth, set out to conquer the world, it embarked on an adventure whose development was too vast to fall within the view of a single generation, and yet its consciousness of its own mission gave it a conviction of essential unity of that development.

No one else ever born has been like Joseph, the leader of his brothers, the prop of his people, who confirmed the dream of his own and proved himself faithful under ordeal by his brothers who saw him as a desperate man that is exaggerating his dream that sold him as a slave to traders who took Joseph to Egypt and sold him to Potiphar whose wife accused Joseph of rape for rejecting to shut up and listen to her uncontrolled sex desires that put him in gaol; Christian sex frees you to love completely. It lets you be fully human. The Catholic Church boldly declares that sex is an extremely good thing - a holy thing! The truth about Christian sex is one of the Roman Catholic Church's general beauty and chastity teachings. Just remember what it's really about: freedom! Pope John Paul II gave us an extraordinary gift: the *Theology of the Body*. His reflections help us see God's original plan for sex and marriage. But more than that....it helps us start to live that plan now! Knowing this plan teaches us what it means to be human. Christian sex is about living fully in the light of God's truth. How we look at and live our sexuality reveals ourdeep convictions about: who we are; who God is; what love is and what it really means, *real love that never leaves, love that never disappoints, love that is never betrayed, and love that is never limited by space or time*; and how society and even the universe are ordered. Pope John Paul II's Theology of the Body looks deeply at the Genesis stories of the creation of man. Genesis describes God's original plan for marriage, including the sexual union of man and woman in which we "become one flesh." The Pope sees this as the key to discovering "the meaning of the whole of existence, the meaning of life." God built into our very bodies his call to love as he loves. That's why we're created male and female, and are built to become "one flesh." The essential things to examine are your intentions and the circumstances.

Catholic sex must always be a truly loving, free act. And let there be no upsets on the way, but enough gentleness in thought, word and touch. "This is why a man leaves his father and mother and becomes attached to his wife, and they become one flesh. Now, both of them were naked, the man and his wife, but they felt no shame before each other." Genesis 2:24-25. Progressive togetherness; they increase in stature, wisdom, in favor with God and humanity. This brings quality in guidance, security and power for long life, riches and honor of the family's territory. During his time as a professor, Sternberg emphasized his research in the fields of intelligence, creativity, wisdom, leadership, thinking styles, ethical reasoning, love, and hate.

In the context of interpersonal relationships, "the three components of love, according to the triangular theory, are an intimacy component, a passion component, and a decision/commitment component." Love is complicated, arising in many forms. We may also experience different aspects of love at different stages of a relationship, and move in and out of various types of love over time. Let's take a look at a few possibilities. Passionate love; Early love is marked by the infatuation of "passion." Giddy, and intense with longing, the lovebirds feel the heart-thumping arousal of the yearning heart. Can't eat, can't sleep. (Why let sleep come between you and the "high" that attaches to thoughts of your beloved?). These are turbulent times, marked by ecstasy and fulfillment when loved is returned; but sadness and despair when it is not. Intimacy; Love may also emerge as intimacy, marked by warmth, closeness and connectedness. Each partner wants to give and receive emotional support and share their innermost thoughts and experiences. If the couple feels intimate, but lacks passion, the relationship is more of a liking/friendship sort than romantic love. Commitment; Sometimes partners commit to stay together and maintain love and relationship through thick and thin. But this love is more compassionate than passionate. When a couple is committed but lack passion and intimacy, their relationship may be stagnant, lacking the emotional involvement and attraction they once had. When nothing but duty keeps them together, this is "empty love." But in places where marriages are arranged a couple might start with nothing but commitment, yet over time become intimate or passionate, or both. So sometimes "empty love" can be the beginning rather than the end.

Consummate love: intimacy + passion + commitment; these different sorts of love may arise in various combinations. Romantic love can be full of passion *and* intimacy yet lack commitment. Companionate love can involve intimacy and commitment but lack passion. Or perhaps a couple experiences passion and commitment, yet still lack deep intimacy. When all three pillars of love combine into the perfect blend of intimacy, passion, and commitment, "consummate love" arises in what many feel is the best of all worlds.

Human mating strategies: In evolutionary psychology and behavioral ecology, human mating strategies are a set of behaviors used by individuals to attract, select, and retain mates. Mating strategies overlap with reproductive strategies, which encompass a broader set of behaviors involving the timing of reproduction and the trade-off between quantity and quality of offspring. Evolutionary psychologists have predicted that men will generally place a greater value on youth and physical attractiveness in a mate than will women. Men who preferentially mated with healthy, fertile, and reproductively valuable women would have left more descendants. Since men's reproductive value does not decline as steeply with age as does women's, women are not expected to exhibit as strong of a preference for youth in a mate. Evolutionary psychologists have also predicted that women will be relatively more attracted to ambition and social status in a mate because these characteristics are associated with men's access to resources. Some sex differences in mate preferences may be attenuated by national levels of gender equity and gender empowerment_. Cultural variations in mate preference can be due to the evolved differences between males and females of a culture. For example, as women gain more access to resources their mate preferences change. Finding a mate with resources becomes less of a priority and a mate with domestic skills is more important. As women's access to resources varies between cultures, so does mate preference.

> *Rachael, the mother of Joseph 'God has taken away my disgrace', was shapely and beautiful, and Jacob had fallen in love with Rachael. So Jacob worked for seven years for Rachael, and they seemed to him like a few days because he loved her so much. He worked for Laban for another seven years for Laban to give him his daughter Rachael. And Jacob said to Laban, "In the daytime the heat devoured me, and frost at night; I never had a good night's sleep. It was like this for the twenty years I spent in your household. Fourteen years I slaved for you for your two daughters, and six years for your flock, since*

you changed my wages ten times over". (Genesis 29-31).

Hymn: **Love divine, all loves excelling**

Love divine, all loves excelling, joy of heaven, to earth come down, fix in us thy humble dwelling, all thy faithful mercies crown. Jesu, thou art all compassion, pure unbounded love thou art; visit us with thy salvation,...
Blaenwern Charles Wesley (1707–88)
William Penfro Rowlands (1860–1937)
arranged by James O'Donnell

Redamancy is the act of reciprocal love; the act of loving in return; a love returned in full; an act of loving the one who loves you. Love may be understood as a function to keep human beings together against menaces and to facilitate the continuation of the species. Unrequited love or one-sided love is love that is not openly reciprocated or understood. *Dalai Lama* says strong action on climate change is a human and sensitivity over fragile *ecosystem*, must be robust.

The duties of love (Jude 20-23): But you, my dear friends, must build yourselves up on the foundation of your most holy faith, praying in the Holy Spirit; keep yourselves within the love of God and wait for the mercy of our Lord Jesus Christ to give you eternal life. To some you must be compassionate because they are wavering; others you must save by snatching them from the fire; to others again you must be compassionate but wary, hating even the tunic stained by their bodies.

Joseph's bones received a visitation; everything is possible for one who believes that personality and environmental adjustment are the better options in rainy and drought seasons! He consistently worked hard when he was a slave in a Potiphar's household and he did the same when he was falsely accused and placed in gaol. He worked diligently there too and he basically became the head over the prison later on, he would make things happen. How many of us would have stopped working diligently because of where we were (pro bono or unpaid internship) or because we got little or no pay?Joseph told Pharaoh what his dreams meant and Pharaoh was so impressed he made Joseph governor of all Egypt when he was thirty years old. The entire country paid homage to Tzophenath Paneach, and he soon became very popular among the people of Egypt. The famine became bad everywhere in Egypt, so Joseph opened the storehouses and sold the grain to the Egyptians. Since Joseph was governor of all Egypt and in charge of selling grain to all the people, it was to him that his brothers came. The day Joseph was proclaimed governor of Egypt was one of the most wonderful days in his life.There is something good about experience. It steadies you and stops you from unnecessary panic or excitement at everything and every idea. We are not jumpy and we do not easily lose it. We remain calm even under the greatest pressure because experience provides one with shock absorbers and grace under pressure.So Joseph is my pacemaker. One and all have got heroes or heroines in life, find the noblest person you can find, and make that person your blueprint and role model.Finally, the extended story of Joseph shows that God is able to save his people in Egypt through the very man they had rejected and sold into slavery.

Then I thought about Dr. James Mwangi, the Equity Bank CEO and Chairman of Kenya Vision 2030, whose early life seemed like mine, fishing in River Mathioya and me River Nyando and both keeping rabbits. Equally we both wake up at 03:00 am and go sleep at 10:00 pm daily; Missionary Youth Movement mentors; and maybe newsletter editors. Like James, my mission is to secure livelihoods, environmental protection, and access to resources.

Our present crises-be they economic, food-related, environment or social-are ultimately also value crises, all of them are interrelated. They require us to rethink the path which we are traveling together as a community. Specifically, they call for a lifestyle marked by sobriety and solidarity, with new values and forms of engagement, one which focuses confidently and courageously on strategies that actually work, while decisively rejecting those that have failed. Only then can the current crisis become an opportunity for discernment and new strategic planning. Suitable community development centered on self-help programmes should be explored, as well as implementation of appropriate policies for lead battery disposal and for strengthening the linkage between combating lead in paint and overcoming illiteracy and ill-health.

In conclusion, Mrs. Okiro did not only tell us stories under trees, but also taught the important of caring for the indigenous trees as they enhance the atmosphere and reduce pollution. However, all of these activities are vulnerable to changes in climate, the environment and related social issues, including health risks from pollution and epidemics. For example, the so called 'water towers' - Mau Forest Complex, Mount Kenya, the Aberdares, Mount Elgon and Cherangani - provide 75 per cent of the country's renewable surface water.

Normally these forests store water in the rainy season and release it slowly during dry periods. So, in addition to supplying timber, fuel and tourism opportunities, they support sectors like agriculture, fishing and electricity. But, when you break that cycle, deforestation costs the economy more than 4 times the cash revenue it generates. In the dry season it reduces rivers flows, hitting irrigation and nearly half of Kenya's power source; in the wet season it erodes soils, reduces water quality and increases health risks like malaria; and of course, it adds to climate change by removing critical carbon storage, which in turn feeds into a much bigger pattern of risk. In fact, Kenya's National Climate Change Action Plan estimates that extreme climatic events could cost the economy up to $500 million a year - a figure which could more than double by the end of the decade. On a national level, Kenya is already home to some of Africa's largest privately funded renewable energy projects, including the $870 million Lake Turkana wind power project and the $620 million OrPower 4 geothermal power plants. I can also see the determination of Prof. Shellemiah Okoth Keya, Chancellor-Dedan Kimathi University of Technology, to promote coffee, tea, wheat and dairy farmers, and hear the concern of Prof., Eng. P.N. Kioni, Vice Chancellor-Dedan Kimathi University of Technology (DeKUT) to progress wind power research and production in the Horn of Africa. For the first time in Kenya's history, a power purchase agreement signed between Strathmore University and Kenya Power, has heralded the commercialisation of solar power in the country in the new 20-year power purchase agreement (PPA). This is creating an amazing entrepreneurial culture, which means that some unique clean energy solutions are emerging from Kenya - innovations the rest of the world can learn from. Like M-KOPA which provides "pay-as-you-go" off-grid solar energy that is necessary and sufficient for lighting, phone charging and a radio. Or the Solar Backpack, which needs just a few hours of sun to provide 8 hours of LED lighting, cutting some of the kerosene use that kills thousands every day. Kenya's nuclear electricity intentions are built on sound premises with the first nuclear power plant with a capacity of 1,000MW projected for commissioning in 2027. This is expected to rise to 4,000MW by 2035 from a total of four nuclear power plants.

Stepping-stones

Judith Jebichii Tuwei, a young woman of uncommon intellectual and artistic attainments. Judith is a stute Kenyan with flawless work values; highly articulation for women's and children's education, including girl-child education scholarships, the elimination of school related gender based violence, environmental protection, access to resources, secure livelihoods, the campaign for youth and women financial literacy and entrepreneurship, as seen in The Equity Group Bank and The Equity Group Foundation. Judy's hobbies are running and swimming- a perfect reflection of why Nandi County is the genuine source of champions. This has been reinforced by the fact that Nandi has from time immemorial been regarded as the traditional cradle and home of sports men and women. It is worth noting that sports has shaped up the history of Nandi Hills from the days of the legendary athlete, Dr Kipchoge Keino, to the now likes of YouTube athlete Julius Yego the lancer, marathoner Eliud Kipchoge, who won 2016 Global marathon Majors, and their counterpart Jemima Sumgong. In July 2016, Kenya national rugby team was hosted in Nandi's Bears Club ahead of the International competitions in Rio Brazil. However, the discovery, development and nurturing of talents is a huge investment. It calls for improvements of standards of coaching, modern facilities and financial support to harness talents from the grassroots. Judith's father David Tuwei has been leading in that journey of transformation through the management of Kapsabet Nandi Water and Sanitation Company that supports the purple tea production, agroecology processing, and dairy farming.

The following suggestions are intended to help you shop without damaging ecosystem:
- ❖ Remember that 'natural' products are not the things to buy! These include plants or animals from the wild or goods derived from endangered species.
- ❖ When on holiday, check before you buy plant and animal products. Don't buy trinkets or goods made from coral, tortoiseshell or other endangered species.
- ❖ When travelling abroad, think before you eat. It is a great part of the travelling experience to try exotic foods, but find out where the meat comes from, and

avoid meat that comes from endangered species.
- ❖ Are you crazy for sea-food? Choose fish that comes from sustainable stocks, such as those with the Marine Stewardship Council label. Nearly 70% of the world's fish stocks are now fully fished, over-fished or depleted.
- ❖ Choose 'fair trade' products (e.g. a number of manufacturers now offer chocolate and coffee that conserve the forest, do not use child labour or chemicals, and give the farmer a fair decent price).

Value #2: Faith Focuses

Faith is unyielding confidence in a person working towards a worthy goal realization. Teacher's hall of faith develops tools and incentives, provide capacity building for achieving sustainable lifestyles and disseminating scenarios for sustainable carbon lifestyles.

>Magdalene Mwanzia Ndunge was born in Matuu, Kenya. Like many form students, she became rebellious to her mother. As she thought she was fighting for her justice and freedom. Being a day scholar, she constantly had quarrels with her mother for poor time management. She dropped out of school. Her father did not blame her, but instead took her to Thika Town where he lived with her and she agreed to join another school two terms later and repeated form two with the guidance from her class-teacher who told that he believed in her academic potentials. Mwanzia got a grade B in Kenya Certificate of Secondary Education (KCSE) Results; she joined Moi University and graduated in 2007 with a Bachelor Degree in Education.

Mwanzia played a very substantial role to Advance Africa in the Kenya national action plan implementation matrix (2016-2018):

> Pillar 1: Participation and Promotion,
> Pillar 2: Prevention,
> Pillar 3: Protection, and
> Pillar 4: Relief and Recovery;

for the implementation of the United Nations (UN) Security Council Resolution 1325 and related resolutions. "*Peace is inextricably linked with equality between women and men...and if women are to play an equal part in maintaining peace, they must be empowered politically and economically, and represented adequately at the levels of decision making, at the pre-conflict stage and during hostilities, as well as at the point of peacekeeping, peacebuilding, reconciliation, and reconstruction.*" UN Security Council statement to the press, 8 March 2000.

"Every failure is a blessing in disguise, providing it teaches some needed lesson one could not have learned without it. Most so-called Failures are only temporary defeats," Napoleon Hill in his book, *The Law of Success*.

Douglas Obed Okindo was born in South Mugirango Constituency, Kenya. His mother bred goats. He moved the goats from their shed to grazing every morning before heading to his primary school. As it often happens most of the time, he had to clean his legs on dew and fearing, the teacher on duty who summon him for his dirty legs; he would sneak through the fence and jump in the class through the backward window. He was caught one morning. The teacher did punish him, but sought to understand why he had to behave that way. After listening to his narrative, the teacher you have:
➢ The same value as all the other children
➢ The right to say what you think
➢ The right to learn lots of things
➢ The right to play

In 1995, he began my studies with eagerness. Before him he saw a new world opening in beauty and light, and he felt within him the capacity to know all things. In the wonderland of Mind he should be as free as another [with the best learning conditions]. The class seemed filled with the spirit of the great and wise, and he thought the teachers were the embodiment of wisdom...soon discovered that school was quite the romantic lyceum as his mother had imagined the daily night prayers. He proceeded to high school and got grade A in KSCE results. "I remember my mother's prayers and they have always followed me. They have clung to me all my life." - *Abraham Lincoln.*

Obed graduated with Bachelor Degree in Law from Moi University in December 2008; his was much influenced by UN Convention on the Rights of the Child, adopted on 20 November 1989. The Convention says that:

- All children have the same rights
- Adults have to think what is best for the children when they decide about things
- All children have right to live and develop
- All children have right to say what they think and to be respected

Most rottenly, many of the dreams that children and young people, all over the world, become beautifully less and fade into the light of common day as both parents and teachers create doubt, disbelief and delays. Gradually children and young people begin to find that there are challenges in their ecosystems. The one they feel most is lack of time from teachers, both at home and in school. At home we would sit together of an evening and listen to the inner melodies of the spirit, which one hears only in leisure moments when the words of some loved poet touch a deep, sweet chord in the soul that until then had been silent. In school there is time to commune with one's thoughts. One goes to school to learn values. When one enters the portals of learning, one leaves the dearest pleasures – solitude, books and imagination – outside with the whispering pines. I suppose children and young people ought to find some comfort in the thought that they are laying up treasures for future enjoyment; children and young people provident enough not to prefer present joy to hoarding an imaginary country rich and broad, a country flowing with milk and honey against a rainy ecosystem days of global prominence as crucial issues such as peace, poverty, health, security, finance and trade.

I was once teased in my class five by other pupils who made jokes that I had helmeted head that helped me to master and remember Geographical features. Indeed Mr. Ouma "Chap Chap" Opuko, our Geography teacher, observed that I had a long-established style of adventuring, learning and a fun of nature. I can remember one drawing the map of Africa and then locating all the rivers without missing any. In a surprise, the teacher said, "You are robust young man and cool-witted pupil with a ladder of strong performances after strong performances: You are calm, steady, imperturbable and composed;

likely to be curious, analytical, reflective, imaginative and creative; and likely to be objective, tough-minded, frank and direct with others, like Maurice Strong, the first executive director of the United Nations Environment Programme (UNEP) and United Nations pioneer in green diplomacy. Maurice Strong's run the world and helped usher in a new era of international environmental diplomacy at the 1972 Stockholm Conference."

With much choice to serve as class prefect than to take more time to read, my mind started to slip away. I met the competition of my life from Nelea Awuor and Susan Kadu. First term, I was second to Susan. Second term, I was third, being led by Nelea with Susan being second. I ranked third position.

Having been relegated, I went to my class teacher Mrs. Owino Millicent and told her that I did not want to be the class prefect as I felt that my problems were arising from class responsibilities coupled with bullies from mature pupils who were repeating the grade. She refused to relieve me of his duties. She gave faith by letting me realize that leadership is not about never falling, but rising up, dusting off yourself and getting on with it. That when a man or a woman has the conviction that he or she is doing the work God gave him or her to do, there is a zeal and a courage in his or her soul that all the forces of this world cannot destroy.

That it is her unyielding faith that in the face all impossible odds those who love their lives can change them. "For, after all, everyone who wishes to gain true knowledge must climb the Hill Difficulty alone, and since there is no royal road to the summit, he must zigzag it in his own way. You slip back many times, you fall, you stand still, you run against the edge of hidden obstacles, you lose loose temper and find it again and keep it better, you trudge on, you gain a little, you feel encouraged, you get more eager and climb higher and begin to see the widening horizon. Every struggle is a victory. One more effort and you reach the luminous cloud, the blue depths of the sky, and the uplands of your desire," responded, Mrs. Owino.

Mrs. Owino was effective with her time in conversations with pupils about our academic progress, sitting with social services to talk about pupils' social-emotional development, meetings with colleagues about latest pedagogical practices and standards, pre- and post-observation conversations with administrators, organized department meetings to look more closely at pupils work, kind and sympathetic, challenged pupils to learn, need centered, recognized individual differences, well planned and systematic, creative, dynamic, and interesting. She also used anti-bullying interventions that she had developed to reduce and respond to school bullying. They were whole-school approaches that combined teacher training, school rules and sanctions, classroom curricula, mediation training, individual counselling and materials for parents. She advised me to use safe and accessible reporting mechanisms to protect the rights and welfare of children who have experienced violence at school. She gave me "better way." She refused to allow me to fail. She said to me, 'Go out and be faithful. Just believe you can' as she handed a book to me. In the book she wrote stories of greatest world leaders of all time.

The "idea" for creating the United Nations was born a few years before the First World War. The idea was named "League of Nations" and came from a book of fiction called "*Phillip Dru: Administrator*". The author was U.S President Woodrow Wilson's socialist right hand man, Colonel House. House later admitted the book was fact presented as fiction. The formation of the United Nations can best be illustrated by prophet Ezekiel's prophesy (Ezekiel 37: 15-28) - The word of Yahweh was addressed to me as follows, 'Son of man, take a stick and write on it, "Judah and those Israelites loyal to him." Take another stick and write on it, "Joseph (Ephraim's wood) and all the House of Israel loyal to him." 'Join one to the other to make a single piece of wood, a single stick in your hand. And when the members of your nation say, "Will you not tell us what you mean?" say, "The Lord Yahweh says this: I am taking the stick of Joseph (now in Ephraim's hand) and those tribes of Israel loyal to him and shall join them to the stick of Judah. I shall make one stick out of the two, a single stick in my hand." 'When the pieces of wood you have written on are in your hand in full sight of them, say, "The Lord Yahweh says this: I shall take the Israelites from the nations where they have gone. I shall gather them together from everywhere and bring them home to their own soil. I shall make them into one nation in the country, on the mountains of Israel, and one king is to be king of them all; they will no longer form two nations, nor be two separate kingdoms. They will no longer defile themselves with their foul idols, their horrors and any of their crimes. I shall save them from the acts of infidelity which they have committed and shall cleanse them; they will be my people and I shall be their God. My servant David will reign over them, one shepherd for all; they will follow my judgments, respect my laws and practice them. They will live in the country which I gave to my servant Jacob, the country in which your ancestors lived. They will live in it, they, their children, their children's children, forever. David my servant is to be their prince forever. I shall make a covenant of peace with them, an eternal covenant with them. I shall resettle them and make them grow; I shall set my sanctuary among them forever. I shall make my home above them; I shall be their God, and they will be my people. And the nations will know that I am Yahweh the sanctifier of Israel, when my sanctuary is with them forever."

The faith in manifestation: Dag Hammarskjöld, the UN Secretary General writes, for example, "We are not permitted to choose the frame of our destiny, but what we put into it is ours. He who wills adventure will experience it – according to the measure of his courage. He who wills sacrifice will be sacrificed – according to the measure of his purity of heart." Hammarskjöld is stating "In our age, the road to holiness necessarily passes through the world of action." The early Egyptians were demonstrably familiar with the science of manifestation; the Bible is quite clear about the manifestation process - ask and it shall be. The first modern rendering of the ideas of manifestation was in a book by an author named Napoleon Hill, writing in the 1930s, at a time when the Great Depression was destroying millions of homes and livelihoods all over America. Napoleon summed up the main ideas of this Active Co-Creation process in his book "Think and Grow Rich." Visualization or meditation are processes which require you to enter a slightly altered state – one in which your brainwave frequencies slowly down into the Alpha frequency range of 7 to 14 cycles per second (cps). The core factor is always to start with a definite goal in mind.

Herodotus was a man who was not afraid, either in philosophy or in war, to embark on forlorn hopes. He is often referred to as "The Father of History". He was the first historian known to have broken from Homeric tradition to treat historical subjects as a method of investigation—specifically, by collecting his materials systematically and critically, and then arranging them into a historiographic narrative. Socrates brought philosophy down from heaven to earth by insisting that he himself knew nothing, and inventing a technique whereby, through skillful questioning, knowledge could be generated in the minds of others as ignorant as himself. Knowledge of human affairs: in particular, of the moral ideas that guide human conduct. Herodotus and Socrates were the great innovating geniuses and the fifth century giants; men of stature. The Greek mind tended to harden and narrow itself in its anti-historical tendency. The genius of Herodotus triumphed over that tendency. The style of Herodotus is easy, spontaneous and convincing. What chiefly interests Herodotus is the events themselves. Hippocrates was not only the father of medicine, he was also the father of psychology, and his influence is evident not only in morbid psychology, but in war-neurosis. Thucydides is the father of psychological history whose chief purpose is to affirm laws, psychological laws which govern the relations between events.

Hugo Grotius laid the foundations for international law, based on natural law. A teenage intellectual prodigy, he was imprisoned for his involvement in the intra-Calvinist disputes of the Dutch Republic, but escaped hidden in a chest of books. He wrote most of his major works in exile in France. It is thought that Hugo Grotius was not the first to formulate the international society doctrine, but he was one of the first to define expressly the idea of one society of states, governed not by force or warfare but by actual laws and mutual agreement to enforce those laws. As Hedley Bull would declare in 1990: "The idea of international society, and to which Grotius propounded was given concrete expression in the Peace of Westphalia and Grotius may be considered the intellectual father of this first general peace settlement of modern times." Additionally, his contributions to Arminian theology provided the seeds for later Arminian-based movements, such as Methodism and Pentecostalism and he is acknowledged as a significant figure in the Arminianism-Calvinism debate. Because of his theological underpinning of free trade, he is also considered an "economic theologist". In The Free Sea (Mare Liberum, published 1609) Grotius formulated the new principle that the sea was international territory and all nations were free to use it for seafaring trade. Grotius also developed a particular view of the atonement of Christ known as the "Governmental" or "Moral government" theory. He theorized that Jesus' sacrificial death occurred in order for the Father to forgive while still maintaining his just rule over the universe. Making the most of this tremendous asset means more investment in education, training, career counseling and placement, decent work, and engaging young people in shaping the future as in "IF" By Rudyard Kipling,

Famous Inspirational Poem:

......If you can talk with crowds and keep your virtue,
Or walk with Kings—nor lose the common touch,
If neither foes nor loving friends can hurt you,
If all men count with you, but none too much:
If you can fill the unforgiving minute
With sixty seconds' worth of distance run,
Yours is the Earth and everything that's in it,
And—which is more—you'll be a Man, my son!

In conclusion, Mrs. Owino was a woman of learning and she groomed me from an early age in a traditional humanist education which would be invaluable in helping me to weather the storm to come. She taught me the important of Kenya's rain forest, including the riverine environment conservation. She taught me that ecosystem service is a new name for an old idea of Plato. Plato, and likely many before him, worried about the environment's capacity to provide sufficient resources for a growing population. In many cases, these worries were expressed as ecosystems degraded; they chronicle a failure of ecosystem service delivery. Recognizing their reliance on natural systems, people have long, often at great cost, on a limited scale, or in constrained locations— leveraging technology assisted learning systems such as Massive Open Online Courses (MOOCs) on functioning ecosystems often goes unrecognized.

Stepping-stones

We should all take care of our bodies by adopting healthier behaviours:

- ❖ If you have a choice, walk through a park rather than along a main road.
- ❖ Repair things rather than throw them away.
- ❖ Remember to exercise regularly; you cannot store up fitness for your old age. Buy produce in season, or even better: buy organic seasonal produce. This will avoid pesticides that threaten both your health and the ecosystem.

Value #3: Prudence Integrates

Prudence disposes reason to discern in every circumstance our true good and to choose the right means for achieving it. Teacher's prudence integrates lifestyle practices across all sectors of society.

One day as a young boy and prefect of class six, I was busy with my regular classroom tasks. One Friday morning I was called by class teacher Mr. Amayo Earlfayo. He was seated under a blue gum tree next to the school's main football pitch, on seeing me; he called three times, "Kennedy, Kennedy, and Kennedy." I answered I am here teacher. He called out again and again. I responded the same way. He paused and then said that an *earl* is a member of the nobility, particularly a chieftain set to rule a territory in a king's stead. He then narrated the story of Christ Jesus disciple Peter of the bible, when Jesus called him three times:

Somehow he narrated Poems by Mary Baker Eddy, p. 14:

Feed My Sheep

…….
Lead Thy lambkins to the fold,
Take them in Thine arms;
Feed the hungry, heal the heart,
Till the morning's beam;
White as wool, ere they depart,
Shepherd, wash them clean.

I seemed to be looking at a sea of crystal suffused with fire, and standing by the lake of glass, those who had fought against the beast and won, singing:

The hymn of Moses and the Lamb

How great and wonderful are all your works,
Lord God Almighty; upright and true are all your ways,
King of nations.
Who does not revere
and glorify your name, O Lord?
For you alone are holy,
and all nations will come and adore you
for the many acts of saving justice you have shown

This reminded me of Joyce from Kamahawa village who repeated class four promising her father to be number one for the rest her classes. What good fortune! I was made the class prefect, based on merit, having been position one in term three of my standard three. Joyce was a beautiful, sleek, and clever young girl. I approached so that we could a form a collaboration of winning team. She replied, "Brother, I have plenty, keep what is yours". I have talents for making high-quality decisions based on limited information, for adjusting to changes in workplace while maintaining a positive demeanor, and for setting goals, monitoring progress, and taking initiative to improve my work. I never gave up hope. I crafted a competitive formula. I proposed my formula to Mrs. Party, my class master like this, 'Madam, I need two assistants, Robert to help me collect books for marking, Jerry to help me keep handwork.' She agreed. Over the weekend, I went to the Homa Bay town and I asked aunt Florence Aoko to buy me an alarm watch. She did. Now I had more time in my hands for personal study and when term one ended, I was position one with 472 marks followed closely by Joyce at position with 470 marks. When the results were read during the closing assembly ceremony, she came to me, pull and pushed my head, gave me her presents of packets of milk 'President Daniel Toroitich Arap Moi's Chego' given to her, and whispered to me that she will never come back to that school again for I had broken her promise to her father. There she went. I have not seen her since. But it d never bothered me so much, I was happy as I was able to limit subjective opinions, criticism and unconstructive feedback from collaborators. My happiness did not last long. One of my class assistants stole my alarm watch. This made me to mistrust people so much as a young person. Over time, I have learned to persuade and influence others to my way of thinking, rather to competitive with people, but to prioritize transformation as opposed to reformation. Joyce was a better option, but even one who took my alarm was too. I value helping others out of their comfort zone to accomplish goals and assist moral imbeciles to modify their abnormal values. Children helping children to stay in school: Since then, I learned about children's rights, the importance of solidarity between children. Before, I did not care about children in my community, whether they were well or not. I became concerned about them and their forums. I visited them frequently and tried to help. One girl by name Bahati from Kakola location dropped out of school because she could not afford to buy books and other items. I made a little money from selling three rabbits, as I reared them. I bought some things for her and she was able to come back to school. I know what it's like in dark times. I know what it's like to have to keep one's hope going through difficult times. I know what it's like to rely on others for support and courage and love in tough times. I know what it's like to have your comrades reach out to you and your neighbours and your fellow citizens and pick you up and put you back in the fight. I am hopeful that all of you are prepared to continue this extraordinary journey we call love. But we are going to have the courage and prudence, the nerve to move in new in a new direction. Thank you! When times are tough we need steady hand on the plough; creating a secure environment for the delivery of the humanitarian aid. The five guiding principles for community child protection are: best interest of the child; be child friendly and gender sensitive; practice non-discrimination; understand and expand choices available to children; and practice diversion and restorative justice.

Mr. Amayo did not just give the prudence to me; he gave to all the children of the world. I am just passing on the gift to others. Having been transformed by this gentleman, I am a strong believer in empowering women. If you give women chance, they will make the world's ecosystems sustainable. I have learned the finer arts of trade as in 1 Thessalonians 5:15-18 "Make sure that people do not try to repay evil for evil; always aim at what is best for each other and for everyone. Always be joyful; pray constantly; and for all things give thanks; this is the will of God for you in Christ Jesus."

People call me 'Mr. Equality' as I gear for equal access, autonomy, choice and emancipation - Gender Mainstreaming. My point in alluding to the allegory of the hornbill is *"The future belongs to those who prepare for it today." - Malcolm X.* Gender mainstreaming is the public policy concept of assessing the different implications for women and men of any planned policy action, including legislation and programmes, in all areas and levels. The concept was first proposed at the 1985 Third World Conference on Women in Nairobi. The idea has been developed in the United Nations development community. On 27 October 2013: To loud applause Sunday afternoon, Dr. Sandra Roberts was confirmed as Southeastern California Conference's next president, making her the first Adventist woman to be elected as a conference president. The history-making vote (567 "yes" to 219 "no" or 72% to 28%) overwhelmingly affirmed the conference nominating committee's recommendation despite a cautionary message from General Conference president Ted N. C. Wilson.

Failure is a blessing in disguise: Sir Mohamed Muktar Jama "Mo" Farah is a British distance runner. On the track, he mostly competes over 5000 metres and 10,000 metres, but has run competitively from 1500 metres to the marathon. Coaches Alan Storey and Mark Rowland made sure that Farah remained competitive and a few words from Paula Radcliffe before the 5000 m final inspired Farah. He has stated that: "She said to me, 'Go out and be brave. Just believe in yourself'."

"There are three kinds of people in the community. The lowest level only believes in their own thoughts, always complaining and causing trouble. Those who are at the next level of maturity seek to find out what others think even though they think they are right. The truly mature tries to follow what others say even though it does not make sense to them. When you reach that maturity, you are at a noble level. Once you have done it, you will think you did well. It will be difficult at first, but try it once and twice. Do not just do things that fit you". From the mind lecture in Sidney Opera House - Pastor Ock Soo Park - founder of the Good News Mission.

To succeed, we must believe in what we are doing. "Believe in yourself and you can achieve greatness in your life". *Judy Blume*

The drop was majorly caused by school related gender based violence. School-related gender-based violence is detrimental to children's education. School-related gender-based violence (SRGBV) is a global concern preventing children, especially girls, exercising their right to a safe, inclusive and quality education. So after graduating from Moi University, I joined Federation of Women Lawyers (FIDA)-Kenya on pro bono basis.

In conclusion, Gender-based violence in and around schools concerns not only the education sector, but also the justice and health sectors, local communities, and those working towards gender equality and child protection more widely. Addressing school-related gender-based violence requires a multi-sectoral approach with collaboration at the district level across education, health and youth and social welfare sectors, as well as cooperation at the national level between ministries. The inclusion of communities will ensure greater programme success and sustainability. Thanks to Betty Odero, the deputy head teacher of Kagimba primary for initiating the Green Belt Movement in the school, where girls and boys planted variety of tree species within the school compound; reinforcing positive messages received by children in schools and clubs organized by teachers in the riverine ecosystem conservation:

Whatever Happens To Me, I Will Try To Do What Is Right

Whatever happens to me,
I will try to do what is right;
I will love the flowers and the sea,
The birds and land animals,
And all that is sacred in life and beauty;
……- *Frederick Douglas Harper*

Stepping-stones

Doing my bit to control climate change and ozone depletion:
- Stop using aerosols (sprays). Although they no longer contain CFCs, they do contain other polluting chemicals and cannot be recycled.
- Ensure that any new fridge contains reduced levels of CFCs or even better.
- Cut down on car/motor vehicle use. Cars are the single biggest source of excess carbon dioxide and produce other greenhouse gases.
- Buy local and seasonal wherever possible. Producing crops out of season means either growing them in greenhouses or importing them, by air.
- Turning the thermostat down by just one degree can save you up to US$58 a year on your heating bill and make a real dent in your household's emissions.
- Turn lights off! For comparison, lighting an empty office overnight can waste the energy required to heat water for 1,000 cups of coffee.

- ❖ Unplug equipment once fully charged. Mobile phones, shavers and electric tooth brushes keep drawing electricity even when the battery is full.

Value #4: Justice Explores

Justice consists in the firm and constant will to give to others their due. Teacher's justice empowers individuals to adopt sustainable lifestyles through education, awareness-raising and participation, encouraging all forms of education. When my mother died in 1996 out of stress related causes and having lost my father in 1989 out of malaria related causes at the Kenyatta National Hospital, I moved from Kano to Kabondo to live with a potato farmer, my aunt Caren Abura, and a catholic catechist uncle, Michael Joseph Olunga Masiko. These teachers participated in the development, implementation and evaluation of the public space programmes; monitor and organize adaptation knowledge-sharing events to analyze programme; review relevant documents and reports; identify problems and issues to be addressed and proposes corrective actions. With my youngest brother Elvince (who for his mettle and intrepidity, niece Grace nicknamed Vincent Kwarula, a Tusker and Kenyan full-back footballer; the heroes who downed Algeria in 1996 'Kenya's finest footballers of all time'), we relocated to Othoro, Kabondo. Thanks for the love of teacher Grace Akinyi Olunga, my aunt's younger daughter, a disciplined negotiator and a proponent of sustainable but focused education, who negotiated our stay at their home. Grace was a unique teacher, her timing was impeccable and her work ethic flawless. Grace can be best described as beautiful, intelligent, focused and astute in ecosystem sustainability issues and solutions. In my primary school years, he attended Otondo Primary School, a public school, for class 7 through class 8; I registered for Kenya Certificate of Primary Examinations from Coffee and Potatoes proceeds. The environmental security has been defined as concerning" the maintenance of the local and planetary biosphere as the essential support system on which all other human enterprises depend." Environmental security encourages a mindset that sees human welfare and the welfare of natural systems as being crucially linked with the seven elements of individual behavior that I learnt from my aunt's family members:

***Personal*:** Grace Akinyi Olunga; that disruption of ecosystems, such as climate change, loss of biodiversity, deforestation, desertification and other erosion problems, depletion of the ozone layer, and various forms of pollution can be mitigated.

***Health*:** Charles Odiwuor Olunga; that a set of issues related to energy, including the depletion of natural resources, various forms of pollution, particularly those involved in the storage and transportation of chemicals, oil, and nuclear materials, and problems of energy scarcities and uneven distribution can be mitigated.

Academic: Alice Akoth Ogada; that the purpose of the pursuit of environmental security is to maintain the ability of society to pursue the good life. That the ultimate purpose of seeking to maximize environmental security is to allow the pursuit of human emancipation, and so there is a particular worth in ecosystem-based adaptation approach to environmental security as it places this at the heart of its analysis and practice.

Work: Elias Olunga; that the effects of human population growth, such as pressures caused by major population movements, excessive consumption and waste, pollution, and overuse of limited natural resources can be best mitigated.

Leisure: Beatrice Auma Mbeche and Grace Awino Atieno; that ecosystem-based adaptation approach to environmental security can help to articulate, shape and justify the beliefs, goals and languages of charcoal practices. Carbon Monoxide (CO): four children (Steve, Cynthia, Wendy and Nancy, all under the age of 16 vomiting from CO poisoning), Grace (in her 30's) and I were overcome by carbon monoxide fumes when cooking chicken using charcoal on a cold Wednesday afternoon. Firefighters were called to clear the kitchen for elevated CO levels shortly before 4 pm. It's very scary. We were transported to a local hospital and we became okay after being helped by volunteers from St John Ambulance First Aid. We were among a dozen of people who were inside the house when the fumes occurred. Those remaining were allowed to go back inside about 40 minutes later. The venting of the building's heating system was found as a potential source. It was changed to a safe range thereafter, but with kids it's still very scary because it may affect them developmentally, that's the worst case.

***Social*:** Michael Joseph Olunga Masiko, Mary Achieng' Olunga, Paul Robert Olunga, Rose Anyango Olunga and Pamela Atieno Olunga; that the carrying capacity is the total patterns of consumption that the Earth's natural systems can support without undergoing degradation. As children, during school vacations, we enjoyed feeding the family's sheep while jumping over their ropes to adventure-fun-learn; when on our bunk bed, Emily, Maureen, Janet and I would say the **PRAYER FOR KENYA**:

"..... *May Kenya ever more find in Christ the Way and the Truth and the Life. May its light shine before the world. And May it always seek the kingdom of God and His justice. O holy Apostle, enlighten, comfort, and bless us all. Amen.*"

***Political*:** Joseph OgadaOlunga; that food scarcities and uneven food distribution, including famine and loss of fertile soils and water resources can be managed.

The Value of a Teacher

In 1998, I gained valuable leadership skills as I was made the prefect of class 8. I closely observed my head teacher Mr. Oyango Kepher's tactics, gaining a keen insight into their strengths and weaknesses that proved invaluable in my life. Kepher demonstrated his toughness and courage in the most difficult situations, including disasters. I developed a command presence—given my size, strength, stamina, and bravery in classroom, I appeared to pupils to be a natural leader and they followed me without question. I learned to organize, train, drill, and discipline his companies. From my observations, readings and conversations with professional officers at the school, I learned the basics of school tactics, as well as a good understanding of problems of organization and logistics. I gained an understanding of overall strategy, especially in locating strategic points. However, my frustrations in dealing with school officials at times led me to stress the advantage of a strong value based, and a vigorous administrative agency that could get results; my dealings gave me the diplomatic skills necessary to negotiate with officials at all levels. I slipped to number 7 by the end of term one in class eight, the worst and the first taste of failure in that school. It hit me hard. My teachers so were disturbed. Mrs. Ouma Jesca being a just teacher offered to coach me on additional subjects free of charge. But she first made me together with the class monitor Daniel Onyango 'Njuguna' who had equally downgraded to mop the whole classroom for a whole week. By the time the third term zonal mock examinations were done, I had overcome my slow start, pulled ahead by a 70 marks margin and I was a clear front-runner I was headed for a better future. Though the margin reduced to 50 marks, history was written; I was position in Kenya Certificate of Primary Education results in our school. It was a new dawn for me. I was selected to join Taranganya High the best Provincial School in Kuria West District, but joined AgoroSare High, the top Provincial School in Rachuonyo District. It was like when nature wants a man by Angela Morgan:

When Nature wants to drill a man
And thrill a man,
And skill a man,
When Nature wants to mould a man
To play the noblest part;
When she yearns with all her heart
To create so great and bold a man
That all the world shall praise- ......

In the words of Prof. Wangari Maathai "There is no more difference between falling and standing, the difference is the willingness to stand up when you are down." The more times you act during your 'window of opportunity', the more likely you are to achieve significantly in your lifespan 'fertile window'. Prof. Wangari was a resilient fighter who worked with international and national partners, providing technical assistance and advisory services for the implementation of environmental policy, and strengthening the environmental management capacity of developing countries and countries with economies in transition. May be you are a butterfly. Dancing improves cardiovascular health and enhances our lung capacity; stimulates the mind, which fights Alzheimer and dementia and increase cognitive acuity among all age groups. Still you may be a cock. Cocks are good racing birds or champion breeders and defend their hens and territories. A good cock is one whose eyes sparkle with fire, which has boldness in demeanor, and freedom. Dog behavior is the internally coordinated responses and generally prefers novelty. Cat has alpha effect, motherly potential, pushing change, territorial size and community aspects. Deer symbolizes the powers in nature. Deer's medicine includes gentleness in word, thought and touch. Deer teaches us to maintain our innocence and gentleness so we can share our open-heartedness with others.

In conclusion, thanks to Mr. Kepher Oyango who introduced the 4K (Kuungana, Kufanya, Kusaidia, Kenya -a cohesive community of producers, manufacturers, and traders working for the good of the community) Club which enhanced resilient agricultural, agro-forestry, pastoral and agro-pastoral production systems to improve community food security; involving me in organizing the planting of over 1000 trees in Otondo primary school, seedlings of which we got from Mambo Leo tree nursery in Nyandolo, over 50 Km away from the school. A weak approach to sustainability integration in a curriculum, for example, involves little more than minimal cosmetic content changes, while a strong approach to sustainability integration in a curriculum will involve use of systemic, inter- and trans-disciplinary approaches, and transformative learning teaching approaches and explicit engagements with values and action. Stephen Stirling provides a useful model for the integration of research, teaching and community engagement to engage pro-actively with sustainability issues and solutions. Transformative learning values shift towards sustainability (integrated social justice-ecological sustainability –economic viability perspectives).

To end, as a self-defined 'general', growth can come with increased responsibilities. A general is an officer of high rank in the army, and in some nations' air forces or marines. The rank of U.S. Army general is the most senior in that branch of the armed services. The duties of a general officer include looking out for the welfare of those under their command, including operations that fall within a geographical area. They hold the responsibility of mission planning and organizing both internal and external military affairs. They are also responsible for maintaining positive morale among their troops and promoting their professional development. General can only be held for so long-through retirement, if satisfactorily service requirements are met, rather than reverting to a lower position of a commander or law enforcer. Army Environmental Policy Institute (AEPI): Defense and Army toward implementing ecosystem management as the part of the Army Environmental Policy conservation technologies.

Stepping-stones

These are simple ways to reduce the amount of waste we produce in our everyday lives. Remember the 5 R's of recycling:
- ❖ Reduce waste by using fewer printer cartridges. Don't print in 'high quality' when you don't need to. Print your docs on both sides of sheets or – when not necessary don't print all (reducing paper consumption and waste).
- ❖ Refuse unnecessary packaging and encourage manufacturers to stop over-packaging their products.
- ❖ Return bottles and refillable containers whenever you can; buy returnable bottles if possible.
- ❖ Reuse and refill as much as you can. Items such as envelopes, bottles and plastic bags can all be reused. Take unwanted clothes to a charity shop-not only are you recycling but someone else will appreciate and benefit from them.
- ❖ Recycle paper, cans and bottles by taking them to your local recycling centre. Compost household waste.

Value #5: Hope Plans

Hope is an optimistic attitude of investing in the dreams of people for positive outcomes related to events and circumstances in one's life or the world at large. As a verb, its definitions include: "expect with confidence" and "to cherish a desire with anticipation". Dr. Barbara L. Frederickson argues that hope comes into its own when crisis looms, opening us to new creative possibilities. Frederickson argues that with great need comes an unusually wide range of ideas, as well as such positive emotions as happiness and joy, courage, and empowerment, drawn from four different areas of oneself: from a cognitive, psychological, social, or physical perspective resulting into power, wisdom, guidance and security. Hopeful people are "like the little engine that could, [because] they keep telling themselves "I believe I can, I believe I can". The psychologist Charles R. Snyder linked hope to the existence of a goal, combined with a determined plan for reaching that goal. Alfred Adler had similarly argued for the centrality of goal-seeking in human psychology, as too had philosophical anthropologists like Ernst Bloch. Snyder also stressed the link between hope and mental willpower, as well as the need for realistic perception of goals, arguing that the difference between hope and optimism was that the former included practical pathways to an improved future. Hope can impact several aspects of life such as health, work, education, and personal meaning. Snyder postulated that there are three main things that make up hopeful thinking:

- *Goals- Approaching life in a goal-oriented way.*
- *Pathways- Finding different ways to achieve your goals.*
- *Agency- Believing that you can instigate change and achieve these goals.*

I suffered from problems with my health throughout my life in High school. In January 1999, I enrolled late and spent four years at Agoro Sare High School for my form 1 through form 4. My cousin Joseph Ogada Olunga, who was a Chairman with Tembo SACCO-Kenya Breweries, paid my school fees while my older brother Joshua Adongo, a businessman provided the pocket money. Throughout my years at Agoro Sare High, I was beset by health problems, culminating in 2000 with my emergency hospitalization at Menelik Hospital in Adams Acarde, Nairobi from May until July.

While in school, while others responded with a cacophony 'frequent use of discords of a harshness and relationship difficult to understand' of funny memes, jokes and comments, I applied the cocktail party effect, the phenomenon of being able to focus one's auditory attention on a particular stimulus while filtering out a range of other stimuli, much the same way that a partygoer can focus on a single conversation in a noisy room; this effect is what allows most people to "tune into" a single voice and "tune out" all others. To get quality results, I also used Premack's principle that has explanatory and predictive power when applied to class performance, and it has been used by therapists practicing applied behavior analysis. Premack's principle suggests that if a person wants to perform a given activity, the person will perform a less desirable activity to get at the more desirable activity; that is, activities may themselves be reinforcers. An individual will be more motivated to perform a particular activity if he knows that he will partake in a more desirable activity as a consequence. Just as "reward" was commonly used to alter behavior long before "reinforcement" was studied experimentally, the Premack principle has long been informally understood and used in a wide variety of circumstances. An example is a mother who says "You have to finish your vegetables (low frequency) before you can eat any ice cream (high frequency)". Though I reported three weeks to the end of term one for my form one classes, I managed number 7 out of 180 students and ranked the best student overall in agriculture. But my secondary school sessions were interrupted by constant chest complications. This adversely affected my classroom performances. By third term of form two I had dropped to position 55, got a 22% in mathematics. Now I had not only to labour, but labour wisely to succeed. The worst crash came in form 3 term 2; I trailed by friends at position 63. When I took the report home I could see the disappointment in my cousin's eyes. But his approach was different. Joseph asked, "How many students did your school take to university this year?" he said sixty. There was silence. Then he asked "if they will take only twenty students next year would you be among them?" I could hear the concern in his voice. He never gave me time to respond. He then continued with a story of his friend's daughter who suffered asthma for twenty, could not attend a boarding school because of her conditions, but still made it to university. He explained further that the lady had overcome her difficulties and was in good health. He shut on the stairs, held my shoulder, smiled, and then said "you are my hope, you can do it, just believe in yourself, I wish you good health and success in life."

At this time I wanted a total focus on the task of winning the future. I wanted teacher's empathy in this battle of dream against fear. Mr.Ochieng' Dennis, my mathematics teacher came in hand to help. His first strategy was to form class study groups depending on mathematical abilities. He placed me in the best group which he called "A materials". He called me later and said he was available to help in case I needed his support. His help was such valuable. My academic pendulum started to swing again towards a brighter future. He gave me hope.

Mr. Dennis adapted St. Augustine's teaching styles to each student's individual learning style. St. Augustine's three different kinds of students are: *the student who has been well-educated by knowledgeable teachers; the student who has had no education; and the student who has had a poor education, but believes himself to be well-educated.* If a student has been well educated in a wide variety of subjects, the teacher must be careful not to repeat what they have already learned, but to challenge the student with material which they do not yet know thoroughly. With the student who has had no education, the teacher must be patient, willing to repeat things until the student understands, and sympathetic. Perhaps the most difficult student, however, is the one with an inferior education who believes he understands something when he does not. Augustine stressed the importance of showing this type of student the difference between "having words and having understanding," and of helping the student to remain humble with his acquisition of knowledge.

Agoro Sare High alumni agree that Mr. Ochieng's remarkable personality was one key to his influence. Although not physically imposing, in one-on-one situations he typically had a hypnotic impact on people and seemingly bent the strongest leaders to his will. Second, his intellectual powers were unrivaled. He had a "photographic memory" for facts, people, events, numbers, mathematical units, and graphs. He devoured statistical information and reports, memorized graphs, and had a perfect recall of a fantastic stock of information. He understood mathematical formulas, but was not an innovator in that regard. He was an innovator in using the financial, bureaucratic, and diplomatic resources of Agoro Sare High. He could quickly organize and integrate all that information, generating brilliant insights on complex situations. He could organize his own thoughts and rapidly dictate a series of complex commands to all his subordinates, keeping in mind where each major unit was expected to be at every future point, and like a chess master, "seeing" the best plays many moves ahead. Combined with his inexhaustible energy, he kept relays of staff and secretaries at work. Unlike many teachers, Mr. Ochieng' did not examine history to ask what anyone else did in a similar situation. Critics said he won many awards simply because of luck; Mr. Ochieng' responded, "Give me lucky students," aware that "luck" comes to leaders who recognize opportunity, and seize it. By 2012, however, Mr. Ochieng' seems to have lost his old verve, and as Angela Noted.

God Knows:
And I said to the man who stood at the gate of the year: "Give me a light that I may tread safely into the unknown."
And he replied:
"Go out into the darkness and put your hand into the Hand of God. That shall be to you better than light and safer than a known way."
So I went forth, and finding the Hand of God, trod gladly into the night. And He led me towards the hills and the breaking of day in the lone East....
(Minnie Louise Haskins)

In May 2007, I went to revitalize the counseling department. I was taken to form two red for introduction to students. Mr. Ochieng' was in the same class teaching mathematics. When he saw me, he told the class, "This is the Kennedy Adongo I always talk about." I was given I hero's welcome. "I like to see a man proud of his country, and I like to see him so live that his country is proud of him."-*Abraham Lincoln.* Ultimately nothing matters very much. The defeat that seems to break your heart today will be but a ripple among the waves of other experiences in the ocean of your life further ahead. The person who sows a single beautiful thought in the mind of another, renders the world a greater service than that rendered by all the faultfinders combined. Honest service cannot come to loss. I have found out what Mr. Ochieng' was doing. He was putting himself ahead in the world by first helping others like me to get ahead.

Today, I am pleased to tell the world about him. He developed the habit of performing more service and better service than that for which he was paid, thereby taking advantage of the Law of Increasing Returns. Truly, no man can rise to fame and fortune without carrying others along with him. Instead of "quitting" mathematics because there were obstacles to master and difficulties to be overcome, I faced the facts and discovered that life, itself, is just one long series of mastery of difficulties and obstacles. Thank you, Mr. Ochieng' for your invaluable guidance during this period. I am also grateful to Emma Mwagi, George Ogonji, Brenda and Kennedy Ong'ondo for profound love.

When my health became frail and dictated my withdrawal from studies, I went home to my guardians, then living in Othoro, Kabondo, where I continued my private studies, here I was greatly encouraged by my niece Lilian Adhiambo Ogada, "All things are possible for one who believes," she said to me while handing over to me a French-English Bible, this made me nurture interest in learning French language. "We can be sure that those whom we help today will help us tomorrow". Eglantyne Jebb, founder of Save the Children, 1928. Joseph Ogada Olunga, former chairman of Tembo Sacco, my cousin who paid my school as my father did to him when in Kuoyo Kochia Secondary School in the 1970s, one evening, while holding my left hand on his right hand and his last born child Michael Olunga on his left hand, Michael Olunga, the Kenya's Harambee Stars striker, he led us to the stairs of his Nairobi residence and sung for us Willie Nelson-Whispering hope:

"Whispering Hope"

Soft as the voice of an Angel, breathing a lesson unheard
Hope with a gentle persuasion, whispers her comforting word
"Wait till the darkness is over, wait till the tempest is done
Hope for the sunshine tomorrow, after the shower is gone"

……

In conclusion, Thanks to Mr. Odoyo Tubman "a man of many letters but of money" for instilling entrepreneurship culture in me and the value of trees in promoting agri-enterprise and conflict resolution; educators can put emphasis on integrated, participatory and bottom-up approaches, giving particular attention to grass-root and community level initiatives, traditional knowledge and practices, as well as to the engagement of key population groups such as women and young people. Ecosystems provide hydrologic services in tandem with a variety of other essential services, including air quality, carbon dioxidesequestration, and soil generation. These services are often interrelated in dynamic and complex ways; understanding their functioning and relationships requires approaches spanning diverse fields of inquiry. For simplicity and appropriate depth of coverage, Tubman focused on hydrologic services, using them as the point of entry to a more general discussion of trade-offs, valuation, and policy. Healthy and functioning ecosystems are fundamental to our present and future well-being. Integrated ecosystems management form an essential part of solutions to sustainable development challenges. The interlinkages and cross-sectoral impacts on ecosystems and environment also come from all aspects of our economic-social activities. While the engagement of high school education in the construction of a global vision and pathway for sustainable development is critical, there is a need for the greater awareness and integration of the ecological foundation and the role of ecosystems in high school education system, across all disciplines. The catalytic impact of interagency approaches and government investment, significant investment in lowering the carbon footprint of high schools, and large-scale efforts to introduce sustainability into the curriculum are leveraging trajectories.

Sweep Over My Soul by Luciano

Sweep over my soul
Sweep over my soul
Though the road in life get rough.....

Oh lord sweep over my soul
Sweep over my soul...

Up With Hope (Down With Dope) by Lucky Dube

I have know this preacherman
For a long time, he was a good man
I have known this judge
For a long time, he was a good man

I have known this teacher
For a long time, he was a good man too
But because of the drugs ......
Them are in loony houses today...

Stepping-stones

If we make efforts to change the way we use water, we can make a difference. The less water a river contains, the more concentrated its pollution becomes. What can we do to save water?

- ❖ Have a shower, not a bath. On average, a bath uses twice as much water as a shower.
- ❖ When replacing toilets and washing machines, ask for models with low water-use.
- ❖ Wash clothes less often. Sometimes clothes are not really dirty, they just need airing or freshening up. Your clothes will last longer too.
- ❖ Never pour household chemicals (such as oil, turpentine and paint remover) down the drain. Choose household cleaning products with ingredients that break down naturally in the environment and do not end up in the sea, do not contaminate water supplies and do not damage people and wildlife.

Value #6: Courage Innovates

"*Courage is resistance* to fear, mastery of fear, not absence of fear." - Mark Twain. Courage assures firmness in difficulties and constancy in the pursuit of the good. Teacher's courage measures and tracks the benefits of action targeting sustainable lifestyles and their contribution to achieving global priority such as ecosystem challenges. "Efforts and *courage* are not enough without purpose and direction." - *John F. Kennedy*. Courage makes sustainable lifestyles a focus in every learning environment possible.

What was important to Mr. Jalang'o, people and their dignity? His classroom was based on mutual respect. He taught his students to respect themselves too. And he taught them to do the very best they could do and to stay true to their inner selves. Mr. Jalang'o stayed true to himself and to the teaching profession.

I found a profile in courage in Mr. Jalang'o who was not my class mathematics teacher, but readily committed to help. He was so passionate and could even make announcement at the school assembly that I see him after the assembly. He would sit down under the tree on tree buttresses in front of our class as he taught me speed and accuracy in solving mathematical problems. He was a teacher of style and substance. I remember when I went to say goodbye after doing my last Kenya Certificate of Secondary Education paper, he said "not now, you cannot shake my hands, until you prove that you are a gentle. If you get "A" in mathematics, come and shake my hands, if not, do not." I got it! I shook his hands. He was so happy.

Courage is the standing army of the soul which keeps it from conquest, pillage and slavery- *Henry van Dyke.* There are those who will consider it their duty, as friends of the Agoro Sare High school alumni, to tell us to revile him, to flee, even from the presence of his memory, to save ourselves by writing him out of the history of our turbulent times. Many will ask what Kennedy finds to honor in that stormy, controversial and bold young captain—and we will smile. They will say that he was a proud peacock—and I will answer and say to them: Did you ever talk to Mr. Jalango'? Did you ever touch him, or have him smile at you? Did you ever really listen to him? Did he ever do a mean thing? Was he ever himself associated with violence or any public disturbance? For if you did you would know him. And if you knew him you would know why I must honor him. Ancient Greeks believed that the flesh of peafowl did not decay after death, so it became a symbol of immortality. This symbolism was adopted by early Christianity, thus many early Christian paintings and mosaics show the peacock. The peacock is still used in the Easter season, especially in the east. The 'eyes' in the peacock's tail feathers symbolise the all-seeing Christian God and – in some interpretations – the Church. A peacock drinking from a vase is used as a symbol of a Christian believer drinking from the waters of eternal life. Mrs. Lillian Muhunsa, my Christian Union School Matron, acted as a trusted mentor, advisor, teacher and a wise counselor. She is the one who taught me about African peacock (the Congo peafowl native only to the Congo Basin) organized knowledge, expressed through intelligent efforts! Sexual selection is the ability of male and female organisms to exert selective forces on each other with regard to mating activity. The strongest driver of sexual selection is gamete size. In general, eggs are bigger than sperm and females produce fewer gametes than males. This leads to eggs being a bigger investment, and therefore to females being choosy about the traits that will be passed on to her offspring by males. The peahen's reproductive success and the likelihood of survival of her chicks are partly dependent on the genotype of the mate. Females generally have more to lose when mating with an inferior male due to her gametes being more costly than the males.

If we expect our students to remember the skills and knowledge we are teaching, we can start by being the type of teacher the students will remember. No effort can be said to be organized unless the individuals engaged in the effort co-ordinate their knowledge and energy in a spirit of perfect harmony. Lack of such harmonious co-ordination of effort is the main cause of practically every student failure.

While he was not my mathematics teacher he did not hesitate to solve any problem, I always had a deep affection for Mr. Jalangó and felt that he had a great ability to put his finger on the existence and root of the problem. He was an eloquent man for his point of view and no one can honestly doubt that Mr. Jalangó was always on his way as he held 'I can *go the distance.*'

"Go the Distance"

I have often dreamed of a far off place
Where a hero's welcome would be waiting for me
Where the crowds will cheer when they see my face
And a voice keeps saying, this is where I'm meant to be

………I will search the world, I will face its harms
'Til I find my hero's welcome, waiting in your arms

(MICHAEL BOLTON)

I worked out a plan for its application that proved to be very effective. At that time I was slowing down in my academic performance. Each night, just before going to sleep, I would shut my eyes and see, in his imagination, a long council table at which I placed (in my imagination) certain well known men whose characteristics I wished to absorb into my own personality. At the end of the table I placed Dr. Sally Kosgei and on either side of the table he placed Prof.

Wangari Maathai. I then proceeded to talk to these imaginary figures that I had seated at my imaginary council table, something after this manner:

Dr. Sally Kosgei: I desire to build in my own character those qualities of African Economic History that integrate environmental efficiency and personnel satisfaction of formal planning and creativity, which were your outstanding characteristics.

Prof. Wangari Maathai: I desire to build in my own character those qualities of a definite purpose and a firm decision to transform that purpose into reality, which were your outstanding characteristics, so as to do the best I can, anytime, anywhere.

Night after night, for many months, this man saw these men seated around that imaginary council table until finally he had imprinted their outstanding characteristics upon his own subconscious mind so clearly that he began to develop a personality which was a composite of their personalities. The subconscious mind may be likened to a magnet, and when it has been vitalized and thoroughly saturated with any definite purpose it has a decided tendency to attract all that is necessary for the fulfilment of that purpose.I started in top ten and was rewarded with a certificate of merit as the best student in agriculture, trailed behind in the process, but finished in top ten. Mr. Maramba Samuel, principal, Agoro Sare High School, rewarded with Ksh. 500 for strong performance in the Kenya Certificate Secondary Examination. With the proper career counseling from Mr. Orinda, the head teacher, Ongoro Primary School, I selected Moi University for a Bachelor of Education (major subjects: history and psychology; minor religion).

In conclusion, thanks to Mrs. Ombura, students nicknamed you butterfly from your walking style. Yes, it was a substance walking style; you showed us how to manage chemicals and wastes from the school's chemistry laboratory. Personally, you showed me how to manufacture sulfuric, nitric and hydrochloric acids in a safe mode; supporting services create the conditions that allow provisioning, regulating, and cultural services to be delivered. I compare you to Mount Kipipiri. The name of the mountain means "butterfly" in the Gikuyu language, a reference to its profile from a distance. In 2005 it was estimated that the forest reserve was home to about 13 elephants. In June 2009 lengthy negotiations were concluded over the alignment of a wildlife corridor between Kipipiri and the main Aberdare Park, with plans to fence the corridor to keep the wildlife, particularly elephants, away from farmers' fields and from poachers.

Stepping-stones

You decide how to spend your money. Choose eco-friendly and more sustainable brands and send a strong message to supermarkets and retailers. A few pointers:
- ❖ Think before you buy. Think about what you need, not what you want.
- ❖ Read the labels: if they don't give you enough clear information, do not be afraid to ask.
- ❖ Select eco-labelled and ethical-labelled products and services.
- ❖ When possible, buy locally produced and seasonal goods.
- ❖ Choose products containing significant percentages of recycled materials or re-manufactured components or that are easily disposable.
- ❖ Buy direct. If you have access to the Internet, shop 'virtually' whenever possible and cut down on transport and transport-linked pollution.

Value #7: Temperance Keys

Temperance moderates the attraction of pleasures, assures the mastery of the will over instincts and provides balance in the use of created goods. Teacher's temperance mobilizes and empowers youths for sustainable lifestyles. Teacher's temperance develops adequate solutions involving all stakeholders, giving particular attention to young people. While youth are surrounded by images and messages about unsustainable consumption, they are also increasingly informed about global issues. Mobilizing youth and helping them to better understand the benefits of adopting more sustainable ways of living is apriority as youth are not only a current but also the next generation of decision-makers and thus key agents of change.

In September 2004, I was admitted in Moi University, Eldoret, where I earned Bachelor of Education in 2008. This degree represents innovation, independence, determination, courage, sincerity and activity. Through my lecturers, the History and Psychology subjects made me energetic, ambitious, charismatic and focused; managing peace, constitutionalism, democratization, the rule of law and the ecosystem sanctity of the human life. As a result of global sea-level rise, storm surges and other factors, economists project that decisions we make today could have a profound impact on the security and culture of the people:

To start with, I want to recognize the warm welcome and oriented the Moi University by the then Vice Chancellor Prof. David Some. I have been attracted to Prof. Some on account of his habit of being agreeable. I still have the photo that made me feel at peace and adapt quickly. Second, I want to be grateful for the guidance accorded to me by Prof. Odhiambo Ndege in liberal policies subject. Third, thank you Prof. Anne Nangulu my history teacher who gave an assignment on a three page summary the biography of Prof. Bethwel Allan Ogot "My Footprint on the Sands of Time." It gave an insight about international developments at UNESCO and most importantly it challenged me to be a bridge-builder of economically, socially and ecologically sustainable development, peace building and humanitarian affairs. Fourth, I was heavily influenced by my African Economic History teacher, Dr. Makana Nicholas who taught the duty of citizens to help the less fortunate and urged his students to enter public service, deepening his leadership awakening. I want to hail Dr. Nicholas Makana for his inspiring history classes. "Get out of the crowd, "as he always repeated. I was profoundly influenced by your diplomacy, vigorous leadership style and reforming zeal. You were my role model. You taught me the duty of citizens to help the less fortunate and public service. I will always love and serve the public.

Fifth, I thank Dr. Ambassador *Paul* Kibiwott *Kurgat*, a Kenya's Independent Electoral and Boundaries *Commission* (*IEBC*) *commissioner* for exposing me to the foreign affairs development and also influencing me to wake early in order to understand and participate in international affairs by watching BBC World News, Aljazeera TV programmes and CNN Broadcasting. Thanks to Dr. Paul Kibiwott Kurgat, I've not only reconnected but have strengthened my connection with the source. God Bless.

The breeze at dawn has secrets to tell you - Jalaluddin Rumi

…….
The breeze at dawn has secrets to tell you.
Don't go back to sleep.
You must ask for what you really want.
Don't go back to sleep.
……..

Dr. Paul Kibiwott Kurgat is the former ambassador to Russia, Ukraine, Belarus and Kazakhstan. Through your history mentorship, I learnt about the term "green liberalism", which was coined, by political philosopher Marcel Wissenburg. Also of the Liberal Party of Canada under Stéphane Dion proposed an ecotax called the Green Shift. The Liberal Democrats (UK) have drawn a "Green

Tax Switch". Equally, after successfully studying Constitutional and Legal History of Kenya, Kenya's Foreign Policy Since Independence, Kenya's Economy Since 1963, and Environmental Education (biodiversity and ecosystem-based adaptation, environmental sciences, natural resource management, natural resource policy, environmental policy, environmental economics) units in my undergraduate class, you guided me to take a Master's of Arts degree in International Studies at the Institute of Diplomacy and International Studies (IDIS) of the University of Nairobi, a period during which I developed an interest in regional integration, environmental issues and politics. Particulars: taking international relations, diplomacy, international law, international political economy, public policy, French, research methods for social sciences, national security studies and gender mainstreaming; the institute is working in collaboration with United Nations University, Ministry of Foreign Affairs Kenya, The Ministry of East African Co-operation of Kenya, The National Defence College, the Defence Staff College, the East African Legislature, the Heinrich Boll Foundation and International Development and Research Centre. Rumi reminds us of the grace in nature - To be awake no matter how short a time is the blessing we all provide to each other. It is that early time in the morning, usually between three and four in the morning. That is the time of the greatest inspiration and creativity, the time when you are the closest to your source.

Sixth, Prof. Jackson Too; at the heart of curriculum transformation towards sustainability lies a transformation in values. Knowledge is not enough to make the transformation to a sustainable world order, for planetary citizenship or for sustainable development. He explicitly draws inspiration from values that promote a better world for all people, and for all living things, now and in future. He argues that all university education is values- based; and that there is a need for more overt engagement with values that promote social justice and equity, human well-being and social-ecological sustainability, and real concern for current and future generations of all living things. In doing this, he challenges 'norms' that have implicitly shaped education systems in the past few hundred years.

Prof. Maria Nzomo, the Director, IDIS, right of the Indian High Commissioner to Kenya addressing participants at the Simulation Exercise on Monday 3rd June 2013. The function took place on 3rd and 4th June 2013 at the Central Catering Unit (CCU) next to the Chancellor's Court and was graced by the presence of the Indian High Commissioner to Kenya. The High Commissioner gave a very informative speech on the actual bilateral relations between India and Kenya. Participants were also given tips on the practical world of diplomacy. The exercise is meant to sensitize the postgraduate students on what will be expected of them in the broad area of diplomacy once they have graduated. The Kenyan Ambassador to the

United Nations Environment Programme (UNEP) Dr. Martin Kimani also attended the function, (idis.uonbi.ac.ke/node/594 or http://idis.uonbi.ac.ke/node/598).

Representing the Foreign Affairs Misnister for Kenya, I sit on the third right of the standing Prof. Maria Nzomo on the bilateral negotiation table, with profound gratitude and great humility, I thank Prof. Ambassador Maria Nzomo, international relations, and master class lecturer, for your kind in teaching about gender equality and to a greater extent gender mainstreaming. Nzomo suggests that ecosystem responsibility should accordingly be broadened away from the state, including upwards to institutions, downwards to local government, and sideways to non-governmental organizations, to public opinion and the press, and to the abstract forces of nature or of the markets. Feminist concept is key to integrating ecosystem values into national and local planning, poverty reduction strategies and accounts. Feminist theory seeks to articulate just those kinds of practices here and now that can be considered emancipating such as ecosystem justice, order, community, security, and mutual satisfaction. Feminist application in ecosystem-based adaptation policy in Africa in general and Kenya in particular is gradually taking root. Research in these areas is calling for increased women political participation and empowerment especially in the current democratization process. For example, Nzomo (1992) was commenting on lack of positive change towards critical women actors in Kenya despite the changing attitudes, exposition of women's invisibility and existence of many women organizations agitating for change observed that democracy in Kenyan society means balanced and harmonious representation of men and women in key decision and policy-making positions (Nzomo, 1992:2).

Increasing women participation in social, environmental and political spheres is offered as the most logical solution to the seeming ecosystem-based security. However, increased participation in the public domain in the absent of policy on gender and environment is far from being a solution to the women's powerlessness in the ecosystem-based adaptation. Therefore, balanced and harmonious representation of both men and women in the environmental security is the only way to secure the works of the Kenyan green ambassador Odero Gogni who negotiated the establishment of the United Nations Environment Programme (UNEP) headquarter in Nairobi or the Kenyan green belt movement leader Prof. Wangari Maathai, a resilient fighter who saved the Uhuru Park for the future generations.

As key role in "social learning" would be the ability of the political elites and global citizens to keep the integration process moving forward. Back Obama: Words Matter "Don't tell me words don't matter. I have a dream-just word. We hold these truths to be self-evident that all men are created equal-just words. We have nothing to fear but fear itself-just words, just speeches. It's true that speeches don't solve all problems, but what is also true is that if we can't inspire our country to believe again, then it doesn't matter how many policies and plans we have..." Thomas *Henry Kendall* (18 April 1839 – 1 August 1882), a nineteenth-century Australian author and bush poet, may refer to statesmen and stateswomen as bellbirds when it comes to issues of nature.

By channels of coolness the echoes are calling,
And down the dim gorges I hear the creek falling:
It lives in the mountain where moss and the sedges
Touch with their beauty the banks and the ledges.
Through breaks of the cedar and sycamore bowers

Struggles the light that is love to the flowers;
And, softer than slumber, and sweeter than singing,
The notes of the bell-birds are running and ringing.

In conclusion, thanks to Fr. Francis Moriasi, the chaplain of Moi University St. Michael Chaplaincy and Catholic Diocese of Eldoret vicar general for the opportunity inthe first year tree orientation through tree planting programme while establishing clear boundaries between farms and the Mau Complex, Ngeria, and Timboroa forests. Ecosystem services are a powerful lens through which to understand human relationships with the environment and to design environmental policy. Ecosystem services are the benefits people obtain from ecosystems. Throughout human history, people have understood that their well-being is related to the functioning of ecosystems around them. Intensifying human impacts on ecosystems worldwide - have accentuated the need to move beyond simple recognition of human dependence on the environment and create more sustainable interactions.

Stepping-stones

Here are some examples of how to save energy in the home:
- ❖ Turn it off! A TV set on standby can still use ¼ of the energy it uses when it is on. In some countries, TV sets do not even have the turn off push anymore: so, in this case, simply unplug your TV set! Switch off lights in empty rooms.
- ❖ Buy energy-efficient, compact fluorescent light-bulbs.
- ❖ Drought-proof doors and windows.
- ❖ Take the stairs, not the lift; it is a great way to get fit!

- Dispose of household chemicals, waste oil and paint correctly: never dispose of them down the drain but use your local council's disposal facilities.
- Compost waste: as well as reducing the burden on landfill sites, compost heaps can provide valuable habitats for wildlife.
- Dispose safely *lead*-acid *batteries* and what causes corrosion, shedding, electrical short, sulfation, dry-out, acid stratification and surface charge.

Sustainability

Earth System refers to Earth's interacting physical, chemical, and biological processes. The system consists of the land, oceans, atmosphere and poles. Population, economy, resource use, energy, development, transport, communication, land use and land cover, urbanization, and more, change the Earth's system. This change is known as 'Global Change.' Global change refers to changes in atmospheric circulation, ocean circulation and climate, the carbon cycle, nitrogen cycle, water cycle, sea ice, sea level, food webs, biological ecosystem, health, fish stocks; humans are altering ecosystems and thereby affecting many of the hydrologic production processes. Understanding how much area—locally, regionally, and globally—is necessary to sustain a particular level of ecosystem service delivery is key to land management decisions.

Triple bottom line refers to the pursuit of balance in economic, social and environmental aspects in the management of an organization. Sustainability is conducting operations in a manner that meets existing needs without compromising the ability of future generations to meet their needs. Sustainability as explained by Antonio Giro "refers to a paradigm from which to articulate new ways of living and of understanding our place in the world". It involves changing cultures, social systems and economies towards harmonious co-existence and equality among people and it also involves changing the way we relate to the non-human world. This requires new knowledge, values and action.

Sustainability goals and strategies of an organization include: integrating sustainability into the organization's strategy and management practices; adopting a holistic approach to economic, social, and environmental issues in the business strategy; focusing on the future sustainability of the organization; taking into account in decision-making, the impact of the organization's operations on the community and the environment; ensuring long term goals are well formulated and subsequently met; focusing on long term talent development; ensuring continuous innovation processes, products and services in such areas as natural resource management, carbon credit initiative utilization, and alternative sources of energy; and prudent financial management practices.

Ecosystems Sustainability values the depth, speed and rhythm of gentleness in thought, word and action; the efficiency with which information is collected, decision-making is organized, tasks are allocated among implementing agencies, the quality of personnel, the integrity and transparency of financial workings of the individuals or governments, including audit functions, and the degree of delegation of responsibilities.

As a result, the School Sustainability Plan is a true School-wide initiative that our entire community needs to invest in making successful. Teachers provide people with educational resources, leadership training, inspiration through various media, art, hands-on activities, and challenges, as well as customized events and programming; an important role in contributing to our transition to a carbon-free future. By generating the ideas and discoveries that will help our school, nation, region, and the world achieve full-scale de-carbonization within this century. For instance, Mrs. Beatrice Ambuso Gose of St Christopher's secondary school, Karen, Nairobi, has been inspiring Kenyan students to plants thousands of trees and winning the "Institution Golden Award" during The TOTAL Eco Challenge Gala Awards 2016 ceremony at The Carnivore Restaurant. In the silence of your own environment, farming and planting seed, tree grows, courtesy of Mr. Julius Ambuso, head teacher Nyakoko Primary of Ombeyi, Kano, Kisumu County, and a courageous father to Beatrice who valued the ecosystem. Go out to love and to serve. Engineers too can enhance ecosystem-based adaptation - wisdom of age and passion of youth. For instance, Jared Mutiso Oda, as the chairman of Kenya Polytechnic students' organization (Technical University of Kenya), a fruit of long candle testimony at the Kenya's Marter Hospital and the Almarai of Kingdom of Saudi Arabia for catalyzing refrigerators that are environmentally efficient, cost effective and resource sustainable;

Almarai is the largest vertically integrated dairy company in the Middle East. Just as Victor Otieno Okeyo, through Kinghorne Limited is facilitating environmentally sustainable institutions, stable regional security, and integrated economic growth. Correspondently, Victor Ouma Ogada and Caren Abura Ogada who have committed Springwell Self-Help Group to build profitable vegetable, potato, fish, banana and rice businesses that create income, opportunity and economic growth to Kenya's rural communities; applying the 'satellite formation flying' concept, that multiple satellites can work together in a group to accomplish the objective of one larger, usually more expensive, satellite. Coordinating smaller satellites has many benefits over single satellites including simpler designs, faster build times, cheaper replacement creating higher redundancy, unprecedented high resolution, and the ability to view research targets from multiple angles or at multiple times.

My Value Footprints

As an environmental educationist at The United Nations Environment Programme (UNEP), Division of Environmental Policy Implementation (DEPI), Environmental Education and Training Unit (EETU); much of my management performance has to do with the mastering of the formulation, actual interpretation and implementation of policies as they impact on power relations. Key among them: accountability, transparency, and good governance; the fruitful multiplication of the law of attraction and manifestation and the filling of the principles of personality and environment. I have deepen, smoothen and widen the cross-sectoral programme outcome and outputs: the development and implementation of the Global Universities Partnership on Education and Sustainability (GUPES), and its three pillars – education, training and networking; the design and delivery of a Massive Open Online Course (MOOC) on Ecosystems Based Disaster Risk Reduction; carrying out research on selected topics such as the strengthening of Environmental Education in the context of the UN Decade of Education for Sustainable Development and the Global Action Plan in Kenya, Switzerland, Korea and China; and implementation of the Eye on Environmental Education Special Initiative, with focus on West Asia. For instance, Ivory Action Plans: trans-boundary cooperation, demand reduction, effective management, healthy ecosystems, co-existence, policy and governance, community co-management, anti-trafficking, anti-corruption, alternative livelihoods, and law enforcement.

There are many different types of plans and planning. But ecosystem's sustainability values strategic planning. Strategic planning is the process of analyzing competitive opportunities and threats, as well as strengths and weaknesses of a system, and then determining how to position the system to compete effectively in its environment. To produce the best fruit requires mastery of work, time, patience and perseverance. Absolute advantage refers to the ability to produce more or better goods and services than somebody. Comparative advantage is the ability of any economic sector to produce goods and services at lower opportunity cost than other economic sectors. Mechanical advantage is a measure of the force amplification achieved by using a tool. Leverage is the ability to influence a system, or an environment in a way that multiplies the outcome of one's efforts without the correspondent increase in the consumption of resources. Leverage is the advantageous condition of having a relatively small amount of cost yield a relatively high level of returns.

UNEP and the Elmolo

The last native speaker of the Elmolo language reportedly died sometime in the 1970s. By then, only a few hundred Elmolo remained, eking out a living on Kenya's southern waters of Lake Turkana as they always had, drinking its brackish waters and fishing for catfish, tilapia, and Nile perch.

Lake Turkana is the largest desert lake in the world and has existed in some form for nearly four million years. Ancient hominids, like the contemporaries of Turkana Boy – the nearly complete skeleton of homo erectus discovered in nearby Nariokotome – fished and lived along its shores. Now, the lake itself, along with the populations that depend on it, are increasingly vulnerable.

The United Nations Environment Programme is facilitating talks between the Kenyan and Ethiopian governments, with the aim of developing an arrangement that takes into consideration both Ethiopia's need for development and the concerns of Elmolo communities living along the Omo.

What If God Was One of Us lyrics by Joan Osborne

What if God was one of us
Just a slob like one of us
Just a stranger on the bus
Trying to make His way home?

……. And yeah, yeah God is great
Yeah, yeah, God is good
Yeah, yeah, yeah, yeah, yeah

Comparative advantage of my involvement are in the United Nations Environment Programme (UNEP) Programme of Work (PoW) 331.3 on Innovations in education on ecosystem services for sustainable development and Sub-programme (SP3) on Ecosystems Management. Leveraging the Government of Kenya (National

Environmental Management Authority, Ministry of Environment and Natural Resources, Ministry of Education, Science and Technology) to develop and mainstream capacity on ecosystem-based adaptation and systems thinking approach execution; Cross-sector awareness and understanding of the importance of biodiversity and ecosystem services for sustainable development is improved through technical support, partnerships and targeted outreach on Sustainability Options.

Introduction of Kenya Green University Network (KGUN) on 5 February 2016 as a mechanical advantage to make performance contract, green curricula, green campus, community and students engagement tasks easier: Understanding and managing ecosystem services requires information about the biophysical nature of services as well as information about their social, economic and ecological dimensions; functionality value of an ecosystem-based adaptation.

United Nations Environment Assembly of the United Nations Environment Programme
Second session
Nairobi, 23–27 May 2016

Agenda item 9: Adoption of the resolutions, decisions and outcome document of the session Cluster 4

> **List of the resolutions under cluster 4 as of 28 April 2016**
> 1. Sustainable and optimal management of natural capital; for sustainable development and poverty eradication **(Botswana, Democratic Republic of Congo, Kenya and Zimbabwe)**
> 2. Illegal trade in wildlife and wildlife products **(Kenya, Botswana, Zimbabwe and other countries;** follow-up to UNEA res. 1/3**)**
> 3. Protection of the environment in areas affected by armed conflict **(Ukraine, Democratic Republic of Congo, Jordan, Iraq and South Sudan)**
> 4. Field based environmental assessment of the effects after the November 2012 and July and August 2014 Wars on Gaza Strip **(Kingdom of Morocco on behalf of the Arab States)**

As Dedan Kimathi University of Technology (DeKUT)- Council Member, in accordance with the LAWS OF KENYA, UNIVERSITIES ACT, NO. 42 OF 2012, Revised Edition 2016 [2015], Published by the National Council for Law Reporting toward Quality Varsity Education in Kenya, I have powers to: manage, supervise and administer the assets of the university in such a manner as best promotes the purpose for which the university is established; determine the provisions to be made for capital and recurrent expenditure and for reserves of the university; receive any grants, donations or endowments on behalf of the university and make legitimate disbursements therefrom; enter into association, collaboration or linkages with other bodies or organizations within or outside Kenya as the university may consider desirable or appropriate and in furtherance of the purpose for which the university is established;

and open a banking account or accounts for the funds of the university. A sovereign can live the ecosystem faith to the full, and that it is precisely these combination-capable and courageous leaders who believe in ecosystem-based adaptation - which draws the greatest blessings on humankind stability, securing peace, teaching order of equality and valuing University Council's lasting prosperity.

Criteria:
- Innovation and creativity
- Visibility and replicability
- Measurable impact on resource conservation
- Impact on furthering sustainability efforts
- Quality of work plan and application

For instance, at a local level, as part of the Kenyan Green University Network, here at Dedan Kimathi University of Technology (DeKUT), we plan to install two wind turbines; a 100kW wind turbine Nairutia firm which is enough for Off-Grid power supply (Kenya Market Assessment for Off-Grid Electrification, October 2015) in rural regions near Nairutia wind corridor and a 10kW wind turbine inside the University to vertically integrate educational activities using new program structures, learning resources, and organizational practices from Bachelors and Masters projects up to Doctoral (PhD) research.

A Legal and Financial Teacher/Mentor/Counsellor

Abura can be best referred to as a Legal and Financial Counsellor. The Legal and financial counsellors provide students with advice and help on issues such as: legal matters; complaint and appeal procedures; student charter; finances; study delay due to special (family related) circumstances, e.g. illness; cancelling your enrolment due to illness or special family circumstances; binding study advice; combining study with a mental or physical disability; and the combination of study and top-class sport.

Abura as Mboya was, strictly speaking, not Luo as such. It is, however, conventionally accepted that his Abasuba people of the Lake Victoria islands have been subsumed into the Luo and are accepted as such. Mboya's intelligence, charm, leadership and oratory skills won him admiration from all over the world. He gave speeches, debates and interviews across the world in favour of Kenya's independence from British colonial rule and spoke at several rallies in favour of the civil rights movement in the United States. In 1958, at the age of 28, Mboya was elected Conference Chairman at the All-African Peoples' Conference convened by Kwame

Nkrumah of Ghana. He helped build the Trade Union Movement in Kenya, Uganda and Tanzania and across Africa. At one time, he served as the Africa Representative to the International Confederation of Free Trade Unions (ICFTU). In May 1959, Mboya called a conference in Lagos, Nigeria to form the first All-Africa ICFTU labour organization. He worked with the then United States Senator John F. Kennedy (later president of the US) and Dr. Martin Luther King, Jr to create education opportunities for African students; in 1959, together with the African-American Students Foundation in the United States, Mboya organized the Airlift Africa project, through which 81 Kenyan students were flown to the U.S. to study at U.S. universities.

A LUO PRAISE SONG

...Dholuo	English
1.	
2. Leah anaweri nyaka tho Ne imiya siling mia koda otamba,	Leah I'll sing your praise until I die you gave me a hundred shillings and a table cloth,
Leah, ing'won, Leah iber, iratego.	Leah you are generous, you are beautiful and hard working.
Leah iloyo mon mathoth Nyako nyar god mesa,	You excel many women The girl from the plateau.

The lyre player sings of Leah's generosity and how good she is as a person. The song may seem simple, but to those who are familiar with the extended family system and African socialism, we realise how much generosity is cherished, as a quality. In verse 2: the player emphasises Leah's other qualities: she is not only generous, but is also beautiful and hard working. Hard work and generosity are qualities that are admired and which parents would like their children to acquire as they grow up. The word 'ber' here does not only mean physical beauty, but also means beauty of conduct and behaviour.

As aunt Tinah Bob Nyambune of Kadiang'a, Nyabondo Plateau, would tell me as a young boy of class six while picking the fallen baobab fruits in her sweet potato and bananas plantation in Nyakach Escarpment or as we went hiking, watching colobus monkey and hippopotamus or to the Odino falls before entering the flood plains of Nyakwere where it drains into the Winam Gulf of Lake Victoria "Anything is possible, anytime, anywhere"; The KENGEN impacts People of Nyanza through Sondu-Miriu River Hydro-Electric Power Project. Kenya contains diverse plant life. Along the Indian Ocean coast are forests containing palm, mangrove, teak, and sandalwood trees. Baobab, euphorbia, and acacia trees dot the lowland plateaus, while extensive tracts of savanna (grassland), interspersed with groves of acacia and some temperate forests, characterize the terrain of the highlands up to about 3,000 m (about 9,000 ft). The higher alpine zone contains giant senecio and lobelia shrubs. Baobab fruit is high in calcium, vitamin C, potassium, magnesium, zinc, vitamin A, thiamin,

B6 and bioflavonoids. It also acts as a prebiotic and is high in fiber. Baobab in parts of Kenya such as Kano plains, Nyabondo plateu, Kilifi and Kitui (and for moringa, Asia as well), these foods offer the potential not only to strengthen local economies, but to encourage conservation and carbon sequestration, too. Managing teams and commercial activities: training of training (ToT) on product secrets, research and innovation, capacity building for institution administrators, managers and leaders, fundraising, extension work and community linkages, project management, product commercialization as done at AVRDC - The World Vegetable Center, Eastern and Southern Africa, Research institute in Singisi, Tanzania are essential ecosystem sustainability mainstreaming behaviors; Buy Kenya Build Kenya as the Kenya Ministry of Industry, Investment and Trade promote local industry through procurement of locally made products. Kisumu Town MP Wilson Ndolo Ayah said the Luo had three goals in 1987: The Umira Kager clan to win the SM Otieno case and bury him in Nyalgunga, his shags, Gor Mahia to win the Mandela Cup, and for Omieri to be returned to Kisumu. Omieri was said to bring blessings, like rain during drought. Omieri attracted local and international tourists, forcing villagers to clear bushes to show if off, and burning Omieri in the process. It was transported to the Nairobi National Park for treatment. Ndolo Ayah's predictions came to pass: Wambui Otieno lost the SM Otieno case, Gor Mahia became the first Kenyan club to lift the Mandela Cup after defeating Tunisia's Esperence at Kasarani Sports Complex in Nairobi. Consequently, the club's anthem, Gor Biro, Yawne Yo! Was tweaked to Gor Biro, Nyalgunga! And after a spirited campaign in Parliament by Nyakach MP Ojwang K'Ombudo who charged that "the Nyakach water supply and a local road have had serious problems since Omieri went to an orphanage in Nairobi," the government transferred Omieri to the Kisumu National Museum for recuperation where it died in 1989 was blamed on its three-month stint in Nairobi, where he missed the ancestral drinking water from River Asawo and the Oduoro stream! Drivers of change are expansion, partners and external environment, including reducing emissions from deforestation and degradation, conservation of forest carbon stocks, sustainable management of forests, and enhancement of forest carbon stocks. Forests impact on climate change here and now and in the future include: increase in global surface temperature; reduction of sea ice extent (three degree world); and reduction in ocean potential of hydrogen (PH; impacts of ocean acidification on marine fauna and ecosystem processes. Forests can act as carbon sources or sinks.

In ecosystem-based (EbA) adaptation a Luo can be compared to 'Hornets Team', a typical example is Joseph Odero Jowi, the man credited with winning world support to have the United Nations Environment Programme (UNEP) situated in Nairobi. It was Odero, then serving as Kenya's Ambassador to the United Nations in New York, who pulled through the unprecedented diplomatic coup in 1972 that saw a major UN agency move – for the first time – outside the United States and Western Europe into the Third World. The feat earned him instant international acclaim. "That was something I worked really hard to win," Odero explains. Obama's father was my student at Maseno," he says. I taught history and geography for two years before going to India to study economics at the University of Calcutta and the University of New Delhi. He continues, "No sooner did I return from India than Tom Mboya asked me to take up an appointment as Principal at the International Confederation of Trade Unions-sponsored African Labour College in Kampala, Uganda. I returned to Kenya in 1963 after a two-year stint in Kampala. I married Salome in the same year." "I was later moved to the Ministry of Finance to deputise James Gichuru. It was from there that I was posted to the East African Community secretariat in Arusha, Tanzania, as Minister for Finance and Administration," he reveals. "President Jomo Kenyatta recalled me after Mboya's assassination in July 1969 to step into his shoes as Minister for Economic Planning and Development. I recommended the late Robert John Ouko to take over from me in Arusha." Kenyatta later appointed him Ambassador to the United Nations where he proved most effective. His diplomatic wizardry in the world body peaked when Kenyatta presided over the inauguration of the UNEP headquarters in Nairobi, unfurling the United Nations flag at Kenyatta International Conference Centre on October 2, 1973. Classified under the biological genus Vespa, hornets are wasps that are in close relation to yellow jackets. Hornets are found across the world in North America, Europe and Africa. However, the majority of these insects are found in tropical climates in Asia. There are 20 species of hornets, hornets benefit the ecosystem.

Personal Experience-The 14th February 2010, Thomson Falls tour with nun Catherine Gathuma, head teacher of St. John Paul II, Nyahuru: Thomson Falls (or Thomson's Falls; also known as Nyahururu) was the name of both the neighboring town as well as the waterfall. The waterfall is said to plunge some 72m on the Ewaso Narok River on the far northern end of the Aberdare Ranges. We were able to view this waterfall from the multitude of viewing areas along the rim of the gorge. Accompanying the overlooks were lots of curio shops as well as lots of locals walking around looking to steer us into their affiliated rose flower shop.

Success in this world is always a matter of individual effort, yet you will only be deceiving yourself if you believe that you can succeed without the co-operation of other people. Success is a matter of individual effort only to the extent that each person must decide, in his or her own mind, what is wanted. This involves the use of "imagination". From this point on, achieving success is a matter of skillfully and tactfully inducing others to co-operate.

Before you can secure co-operation from others; nay, before you have the right to ask for or expect co-operation from other people, you must first show a willingness to co-operate with them. An aim in life is the only fortune worth finding; and it is not to be found in foreign lands, but in the heart itself - *Robert Louis Stevenson.*

Leadership is essential for the attainment of Success, and Initiative is the very foundation upon which this necessary quality of Leadership is built. Initiative is as essential to success as a hub is essential to a wagon wheel. Leadership is something that you must invite yourself into; it will never thrust itself upon you. This is the real value of the teacher to the learner. I got it! Remember that your only limitation is the one that you set up in your own mind. Like Joseph, CHERISH your dreams for they your life's blueprints. SERVICE, Sacrifice and Self-Control are three words which must be well under-stood by the person who succeeds in doing something that is of help to the world. This appeal is necessary to be made to the people of the different nations of the world in support of a universal plan for sustainable development, and this plan must be facilitated upon the minds of the oncoming generations with the same diligent care that sustainability is planted firmly in the minds of the young the ideals of respective value ecosystems.

"Singleness of purpose is one of the chief essentials for success in life, no matter what may be one's aim."-*John D. Rockefeller, Jr.* Rockefeller Foundation work within their 'Revalue Ecosystems' focus on solutions that harness the importance of ecosystems as an asset for smart development, economic and social progress, and long-term resilience; accounting for the significant role nature plays in promoting economic and social well-being.

What do polar bears, hummingbirds, clams, bowhead whales and invasive plant species have to do with Earth science spacecraft orbiting overhead 24/7? Soon observations from the National Aeronautics and Space Administration (NASA)'s Earth-observing satellites of our planet's climate will be brought to bear on understanding how different species and ecosystems respond to climate changes and developing tools to better manage wildlife and natural resources. NASA has joined with the U.S. Geological Survey, National Park Service, U.S. Fish and Wildlife Service and Smithsonian Institution to initiate new research and applications efforts that will bring the global view of climate from space down to Earth to benefit wildlife and key ecosystems Olympic Themes and National or International Themes of the World:

The Value of a Teacher

The Anthem - Tom Conry
We are called, we are chosen.
We are Christ for one another.
We are promised to tomorrow,
while we are for him today.
We are sign, we are wonder,
we are sower, we are seed…..

American National Anthem
Oh, say! can you see by the dawn's early light
What so proudly we hailed at the twilight's last gleaming;
Whose broad stripes and bright stars, through the perilous fight,
O'er the ramparts we watched were so gallantly streaming?
And the rocket's red glare, the bombs bursting in air,…..

Kenya Anthem
O God of all creation
less this our land and nation
Justice be our shield and defender
May we dwell in unity
Peace and liberty
Plenty be found within our borders.

African Union Anthem
Let us all unite and sing together
To uphold the bonds that frame our destiny
Let us dedicate ourselves to fight together
For lasting peace and justice on earth

United Nations Anthem
Holding UN flags, high and unfurled,
We set out on mission 'One World';
Spreading harmony, we unify Europe,
In North America, we resume with hope.

Arousing 'oneness' in South America,
And erasing all boundaries in Africa;
Uniting folks of all colors and regions,
across Asia-the birthplace of religions….

Dan Fogelberg - Earth Anthem Lyrics
And we are but an island in an ocean
This is our home, third from the sun
Let it be evergreen, let it be evergreen....

God, keep it evergreen
To keep it ever green I would lay my life down

And we are but an island in an ocean
This is our home, third from the sun
Let it be evergreen, let it be evergreen

GE'S 150-MW KENYA WIND POWER PROJECT

Kenya's strategic plan to make much more use of renewable energy resources took another step forward on Jan. 30, when Prime Minister Raila Odinga and GE CEO Jeffrey Immelt announced that GE will build a 150-MW wind energy farm in the town of Ngong, 12 miles (19 kms) southwest of Nairobi.

With demand for electricity growing at some 14% per year and the country being heavily reliant on fossil fuel imports, Kenya's keen to develop a range of renewable energy resources to augment hydroelectricity, which produces nearly half of supply, and reduce fossil fuel imports. The Kenyan government has an national renewable energy plan calling for a minimum of 2 GW of electricity from renewable energy sources to be produced by 2013, according to a Bloomberg Business week report. Kenya's ambitious renewable energy strategy highlights the multiple, reinforcing benefits of developing renewable energy resources for developing countries. Situated astride the East African Rift Zone, geothermal power project development has been at the forefront of Kenya's renewable energy development initiative, but the country also has significant wind and solar energy resources, and it's moving forward with plans to develop biogas, biomass, and waste-to-energy projects as well.

THE GREENING OF KENYA: Kenya's forest cover stands between 5-7%; a 17 years old Lilly Tanui of Bunyore Girls, a representative to the Yale Young Global Scholar on Environment and sustainable energy conference at the Yale University is encouraging Kenyans children to embrace ecosystem-based adaptation to save the future generation. Books and lessons, in themselves, are of but little value; their real value, if any, lies not in their printed pages, but in the possible action which they may arouse in the reader by the teacher. You cannot change the course of this law, but you can adapt yourself to its nature and thereby use it as an irresistible power that will carry you to heights of achievement which could not be attained without its aid.

Teacher Jackson Muvevi was thrilled to attend the Green Initiative Awards ceremony for students from St Martin Kaewa Secondary School in Machakos County. In fact, he decided to borrow a green leaf and implement the tree-planting programme in his own school, Tulimyumbu primary, Masinga constituency in Machakos. Muvevi is not only the Green Initiative Challenge teacher but also a champion. He has made sure teachers, students, parents and the community as a whole adopts the initiative.

Regina Mutiswa, 15 has adopted tree planting, saying climate change can only be addressed if everyone plays his or her part. Trees have many benefits: They help to combat climate change by absorbing excess carbon dioxide and reducing the overall concentration of greenhouses gases (nitrogen oxides, ammonia, sulfur dioxide and ozone). This reduces pollution. They also produce oxygen. Trees provide cooling and conserve energy. Their roots prevent soil erosion.

Golden Value Rule
It is simply the Golden Value Rule, embodied in these words: 'Therefore, whatever you want others to do for you do also the same for them, for this are the Law and the Prophets.' Ecosystems and the biological diversity contained within them provide a stream of goods and services, the continued delivery of which remains essential to our economic prosperity and other aspects of our welfare. Ecosystem goods refer to the natural products harvested or used by humans such as wild fruit and nuts, forage, timber, game, natural fibres, medicines and so on. More importantly, ecosystem services support life by regulating essential processes such as purification of air and water, pollination of crops, nutrient cycling,

decomposition of wastes, and generation and renewal of soils, as well as by moderating environmental conditions by stabilising climate, reducing the risk of extreme weather events, mitigating droughts and floods, and protecting soils from erosion. The benefits of these services manifest themselves at local, regional and global scales with often conflicting demands between stakeholders at these different levels.

Driving forces behind ecosystem degradation are many and interlinked. Human society has for centuries taken for granted the services provided by natural systems partly because they are not formally traded and are therefore dissociated from pricing that reflects and warns of changes in supply or demand conditions. Just as markets fail to signal ecosystem degradation, economic policies frequently provide perverse incentives that encourage it. Absence of clearly defined and secure property rights, lack of clear environmental policy goals, poor enforcement of existing regulation, corruption, lack of political will and lack of institutional capacity are examples of failing governance that also leads to ecosystem degradation.

Better information on its own will not bring about sustainable use of ecosystems, achievable only if this information is then used to address the drivers of ecosystem degradation. Examples of measures capable of 'capturing' demonstrated value include payments for provision of ecosystem services, creation of markets for ecosystem services where they do not already exist, improving the property rights system, enhancing the assets of the poor, improving the quality of economic growth, reforming international and industrial country policies and improving governance. Evidence from multiple ecosystems at a variety of temporal and spatial scales, suggests that biological diversity acts to stabilize ecosystem functioning in the face of environmental fluctuation. Variation among species in their response to such fluctuation is an essential requirement for ecosystem stability, as is the presence of species that can compensate for the function of species that are lost.

In order to protect biodiversity, we must change our habits/ way we earn out living. In the U.S., the government offers tax credits to people with solar panels/hybrid automobiles. This is a key milestone on the way to financial freedom: providing you with greater autonomy and freedom of choice. Traditionally, retirement means stopping work for pay, whether in the form of formal retirement, early retirement or semi-retirement. On the other hand, financial freedom means working for passion and purpose alone. Retirement is generally defined as sufficient personal wealth to cover living expenses without accessing assets, but all-encompassing financial freedom means different things to different people. 'How much is enough' is a thoroughly personal question. Every person has his or her own measure of what constitutes peace-of-mind and personal freedom, and the extent of the legacy he or she wish to leave behind.

Teacher's values are levers for change: Mainstreaming ecosystem-based adaptation into learning planning to foster sustainability transitions:

- To promote the resilience of livelihoods;
- To reduce the impacts of natural disasters such as storms and floods, on vulnerable people and ecosystems;
- To build the capacity of civil society and government institutions to support integrated approaches to adaptation;
- To increase awareness of the underlying causes of vulnerability (degraded ecosystems, poor governance, unequal access to resources and services, discrimination and other social injustices);
- To promote the sustainable management and conservation of biodiversity to maintain the benefits provided by ecosystems (e.g. provision of food and shelter).

Addressing the effects of climate change via adaptation measures and the implementation of mitigation measures is central to ensuring continued ecosystem functioning, human health and socio-economic security. Ecosystem-based approaches have emerged as a key instrument to confront these concerns across sectors of business and society, offering multiple benefits in a potentially cost-effective manner.

The concept of an 'ecosystem-based approach' builds on the Convention on Biological Diversity's (CBD) definition, stating that: "the ecosystem approach is a strategy for the integrated management of land, water and living resources that promotes conservation and sustainable use in an equitable way" and which aspires to maintain the natural structure and functioning of ecosystems.

Ecosystem-based approaches address the crucial links between climate change, biodiversity, ecosystem services and sustainable resource management and thus have the potential to simultaneously contribute to the avoidance and reduction of greenhouse gas emissions and the enhancement of sinks - *inter alia* - through increased carbon sequestration. These approaches also maintain existing carbon stocks; regulate water flow and storage, maintain and increase resilience, reduce vulnerability of ecosystems and people, help to adapt to climate change impacts, improve biodiversity conservation, livelihood opportunities, and provide better health and recreational benefits.

Life's circumstances put limits on decisions we can make. However, within those drivers, restraints and trends, we have a wide range of choices to make. I was born in the drought of Kano plain and grew up in the floods of River Nyando. Besides those challenges, I had teachers who built me up and planted me upon values that adjusted my personality to fit my ecosystem and at the same improve my ecosystem to suit my personality. This combination is what gave me the sustainable lifestyle within my environment - hopeful thinking that makes up valuable goals, pathways and agencies to open up a large window of opportunities on air, land, sea and in the capitals of the world. That experience led me to pursue sustainable teaching, green diplomacy and economics; informing my Vision "soaring at the globe", Mission "know, love and serve", Motto "service values", Philosophy "To Yearn Is To Learn", and Brand Statement "Value Creator", Business Models "Partnerships, Co-operations and Networks", Culture "Communication, Education and Training, and Consultation", and Critical Success Factors: "Leverage global system; Market driven and customer-focused; Professional and efficient operations; Brand promotion, protection and projection; and Catalyzing output, outcome and impact in securing livelihoods, environmental protection, and accessing resources."

There is a need for greater integration of ecosystems awareness and systems thinking in the education system, across disciplines as Camelot, a musical by Alan Jay Lerner (book and lyrics) and Frederick Loewe (music) which values the future generations, probably my favorite line is the second line of stanza one as sung by Richard Burton in 1978: *"The climate must be perfect all the year"* as it mitigates national security, law enforcement, and foreign affairs concerns. Camelot teaching form is unique in the willing obedience tradition:

It's true! It's true! The crown has made it clear
The climate must be perfect all the year

A law was made a distant moon ago here
July and August cannot be too hot
And there's a legal limit to the snow here

Ecosystem-based Adaptation was my agenda while carrying out the feasibility study Equity Bank Awendo branch with an archive section in 2012; Mark Manco, Shadrack Malela and I focused ecosystem sustainability first. My most living experience includes a stint at State Corporations; spearheading the development of a 10 year national Master Plan for Science and Technology Parks in Kenya and in particular the (DeKUT) and the proposed National Cancer Hospital at DeKUT Main Campus under President Uhuru Kenyatta directives.

My value message to you as was to David Okinyi, the student whom I mentored at Kanyawanga High School under the Equity Group Foundation – Wings To Fly Mentorship Program which propelled him to BSc in Medicine, Northern Arizona University: "Go do what you want to do. Be who you want to be. Create a life for yourself that you will love with all of your heart, and never lose hope or hesitate to step outside of your comfort zone, because, in the end, the outcome, whatever it may be, is rewarding and leaves you with a good feeling in your heart, because you believe you are preserving environment and maintaining it "for the enjoyment, education, and inspiration of this and future generations."

About the Author

That which is rare has value. Kennedy Onyango Adongo is a Kenyan economist, diplomat and educationist. My Master's Degree in International Studies from the Institute of Diplomacy and International Studies at the University of Nairobi, Bachelor's Degree in Education from Moi University, and North-South, South-South and Triangular Cooperation experience are infinite in value. The diversity of my Luo, Kalenjin, Kisii, Kikuyu and Luhya ancestral heritage adds to my Ecosystem and Systems Thinking Approach, offerings and accomplishments in Swahili, English and French, both on the sustainability of economic growth and pursuit of global environmental sustainability plane

Appendices

1. On 4/19/16, Bianca Notarbartolo wrote:
   Dear Kennedy,
   Many thanks for thinking of me as a reviewer for your amazing work which I read with great interest. I'm afraid I'm not in a position to contribute to this manuscript as I have to admit my ignorance on the topic, but your work gave me the opportunity to think critically about this largely overseen yet incredibly important aspect of our (and our children in the future) life: teachers are indeed the most important figure in a child's life - even more important than the parents' one, I would argue.

   And the fact that you are quoting Rudyard Kipling' poem 'IF' really touched and impressed me, as that one is really dear to my heart since it was dedicated to me by a person very close to me and I have printed it in my house.

   Congratulations on such an amazing - and I'm sure also very tiring - work, and I look forward to hearing of your successes in the future - as I'm sure you will have plenty.

   Bianca

2. On 4/19/16, Ruth Aluodo wrote: Hello Kennedy,

 Actually I can say I am one person who holds teachers in very high esteem. The book brings back those fond memories and the sad ones as well. But what I have noted is that the syllabus limits our teachers to performing to their best and the education system too. I have a lot to say but that paragraph will do for now. I am happy for you and can't wait to get a copy. Do it right and fast!

 Ruth

References

1. Balmford A, Bond W. 2005.Trends in the state of nature and their implications for humanwell-being. Ecol. Lett. 8:1218–34
2. Mooney HA, Ehrlich PR. 1997. Ecosystem services: a fragmentary history.
3. Bass S. 2006. Environment for the MDGS: An IIED Briefing. London: Int. Inst. Econ. Dev.
4. Carpenter SR, DeFries R, Dietz T, Mooney HA, Polasky S, et al. 2006. Millennium Ecosystem Assessment: research needs. Science 314:257–58
5. Feen RH. 1996. Keeping the balance: ancient Greek philosophical concerns with populationand environment. Popul. Environ. 17:447–458
6. Norgaard RB. 1994. Development Betrayed: The End of Progress and a Co-Evolutionary Revisioningof the Future. New York: Routledge
7. Dearmont D, McCarl BA, Tolman DA. 1998. Costs of water treatment due to diminishedwater quality: a case study in Texas. Water Resour. Res. 34:849–53
8. Boyd J, Banzhaf S. 2006. What Are Ecosystem Services? The Need for Standardized Accounting Units. Discuss. Pap. 06–02. Resour. Future, Washington, DC

9. Falkenmark M, Gottschalk L, Lundqvist J, Wouters P. 2004. Towards integrated catchmentmanagement: increasing the dialogue between scientists, policy-makers and stakeholders.Int. J. Water Resour. Dev. 20:297–309
10. Honey, P. & Mumford, A. (1982) Manual of Learning Styles London: P Honey
11. Allaby M., Green Facts. London: Reed, 1989

www.ingramcontent.com/pod-product-compliance
Lightning Source LLC
Chambersburg PA
CBHW030937180526
45163CB00002B/606